Medical handbook for mountaineers

By the same author

Two and Two Halves to Bhutan (1970)
Doctor on Everest (1972)

Medical handbook for mountaineers

Peter Steele

Constable · London

David + Eva

to accompany you on
many adventures.

Peter Steele

Whitehorse Yukon
August 1989

Published in Great Britain 1988
by Constable and Company Limited
10 Orange Street London WC2H 7EG
Copyright © by Peter Steele 1988
First published in Great Britain in 1976
by William Heinemann Medical Books Limited
Set in 9 pt Times by
Rowland Phototypesetting Limited
Bury St Edmunds, Suffolk
Printed in Great Britain by
The Bath Press Limited, Bath, Avon

British Library CIP data
Steele, Peter
Medical handbook for mountaineers
1. First aid – Manuals – For mountaineering
I. Title
616.02′52

ISBN 0 09 468570 3

To Lucy

Contents

Contents

List of diagrams

(Drawings by Jean McAllister)

Acknowledgements

Monty Alford, mountaineer; Steve Bezruchka, Everest doctor; Dave Boon, ENT surgeon; Frank Buffam, ophthalmologist; Jeremy Carless, family physician; Charles Clarke, Everest doctor; Peter Cummings, emergency physician; Peter Currie, anaesthetist; Baman Daver, plastic surgeon; Jim Dalrymple, general surgeon; John Dickinson, physician in Nepal; Andrew Elkington, eye surgeon; Max Fleming, father-in-law; Pam Glassby, dental surgeon; John Hayward, cold physiologist; Tony Holmyard, outdoor educator; Charlie Houston, altitude physician; Judy Isaac-Renton, tropical medicine; John James, family physician; Afan Jones, orienteer; Eric Langmuir, mountaineer; Peter Lord, general surgeon; Hector Mackenzie, mountain guide; Paul Millac, neurologist; Wayne Merry, mountaineer; Bruce Paton, vascular surgeon; Ann Rae, microbiologist; Drummond Rennie, altitude physician; Gil Roberts, Everest doctor; Barney Rosedale, Everest doctor; Sandy Sanders, clinical pharmacologist; Chris Shank, mountaineer; Adam Steele, computer scientist; Ian Taylor, plastic surgeon; Michael Ward, Everest surgeon; Andy Williams, high altitude pilot.

Preface

The aim of this book is to help the active mountaineer on the hills to muster his wits in order to keep the victim of an accident or a medical emergency alive during the first few shattering minutes, and to prevent him worsening before skilled care is reached.

A recurring question of helpful critics is, 'who is your audience?' The book is for anyone who ventures into mountains – a teacher leading schoolchildren on a hike over Snowdon, a maestro on the Brenva Face in the Alps, or a young doctor trekking with a party in the Arun Valley of the Himalaya. Medical knowledge will vary widely, and yet I have written one book in hope of interesting everyone – a dangerous task.

In order to separate information that should be universal from more technical detail, different print sizes are used. This allows matters of interest to the more medically trained reader, or those superfluous to on-the-spot practical help, to be retained in small print without burdening the average person with gobbledegook.

I struggled with the question of how to refer to the injured party – victim, casualty, climber, patient, trekker or person – and settled on victim, whom I also generally refer to as male purely for ease of syntax.

Economy of words, clear meaning and plain English are my foremost aim throughout. I try to avoid medical jargon, the cloak of mystique under which many doctors hide. Occasionally a medical word is apt, and then I am not shy to use it.

Many friends, experts in their own fields, have been generous with their criticism; my debt to them is immense. They have sealed the book with authority and helped me to make it as accurate yet understandable, as possible. Any errors or omissions are my responsibility, but I would greatly appreciate hearing about them.

Introduction

This book aims to help you understand some basic medical principles and, by using limited knowledge, to act intelligently and with common sense in an emergency. Accidents and medical crises create anxiety and tension. Even experienced emergency physicians feel adrenaline coursing through their veins when an ambulance siren wails and strobe lights flash, as they wonder what horror will unfold when the ambulance doors open. In the mountains you will be far from help with few resources and meagre medical knowledge, a situation that will readily cause panic and confusion unless you, the rescuer, keep a cool head and act decisively.

Assess the victim's condition and decide what needs doing immediately in order to prevent him worsening or dying before you can get help. During this lonely, anxious time, the sight of blood and a cadaverous victim may lead you to flounder unless you marshal your thoughts clearly and quickly.

Accident prevention

Prevention, if properly applied, would make this book redundant. In an imperfect world prevention, sadly, will never be totally effective. Mountains are hazardous, and some people will get hurt and may die, whatever precautions are taken. Prevention demands learning new skills in order to reduce the dangers inherent in climbing. Learn everything possible about the wilderness before venturing into it, apply common sense whilst there, and judge when to accept defeat and turn back rather than press on towards disaster. Only a thorough apprenticeship will prepare you to handle these dangers, that can be reduced by developing your technical skills in order to become an all-round mountaineer. Medical problems on mountains are often problems of mountains more than of medicine. It is comparatively easy to splint a broken leg and treat the pain, but how to evacuate the victim safely without suffering from hypothermia or further injury will depend on hard-won skill and experience.

A big medical kit and all the newest gear will not lessen the dangers of mountains. Carry only essentials because, if you are weighed down by impedimenta, energy needed to cope with the unexpected will have been fruitlessly expended.

Emergency doctors can do little outside a hospital. A well-trained first-aider may be more useful in the wilderness than a doctor who is ignorant of the special problems of remote places. An MB (or whatever) after his name does not necessarily mean he is any better than a competent outdoors-man who has learned the basic medical skills. Illnesses are as often cured by Nature as by the doctor.

The law

Good Samaritans in the outdoors are unlikely to fall foul of the law when their attempts to save life fail provided they conscientiously apply skills learned and stick within their capabilities. Legal action looms large these days, so the lily-livered should stay well away from the medical care business. Rescuing, like adventure, carries risks but we still attempt both.

1   Casualty assessment

After an accident one person should take charge in order to prevent
confusion from too many people offering smart ideas. If reluctant to
lead, give your support to a leader who has first-aid experience, and
thereby influence the operation from a back seat.

Plan a safe approach to the victim. In the mountains, for
example, come from below or from the side, but not from above
where you may start a rock-slide or an avalanche. Move the victim
to safe level ground if possible, make a shelter, and keep him warm.
Undo tight clothing and equipment, cutting along seams if
necessary. Do the minimum first-aid on site in order to stabilize him
until skilled medical help is reached. Panicking bystanders put
pressure on a first-aider to *do* something, but knowing what not to
do is more important. Avoid action for action's sake, that may lead
to meddlesome interference. Whatever you may do, not-so-bad
accident victims tend to get better, while bad ones tend to get worse
and die.

Care of the victim

Care means total care of the victim – frightened, anxious, and in
pain – not just bandaging his wounds. First, reassure and comfort
him, especially if it seems he may die. Compassion needs no
medical skill, just warm caring humanity. Call him by name; tell
him your name, who you are and your first-aid qualifications in
order to bolster his confidence. Touching helps to establish a bond
of trust; hold his hand or lay your hand on his shoulder.

Make him as comfortable as the ground will allow; let him pee if
he needs to. While waiting for, and during, the rescue, insulation
from the cold ground below is just as important as piling clothes on
top to keep him warm. An immobile, injured person can quickly
suffer hypothermia, which may be more lethal than his injury.

Moving him may cause pain, so give warning to avoid surprise.
Withhold pain-killers usually until after examining him in order not
to disguise pain and obscure physical signs; but if pain is severe,

treat it regardless. Examine him carefully and thoroughly, thereby reassuring him your care will be thorough, but also lessening the chance of missing some important sign.

Assess the victim and then explain carefully his situation, telling no lies. He will be anxious about being crippled, that his job will be jeopardized, what his family will say. Inevitably he will feel guilty at being the cause of so much trouble; even if the accident was his fault, blaming him is pointless. From now on he will be totally dependent on your rescue skills and such dependence erodes self-esteem. Encourage him to discuss the accident in order to dispel guilt and embarrassment.

Make a plan of action, discuss it with the victim, and try to involve him in his own rescue. He may be able to hold a rope, or light a stove to boil water for tea while you attend to other things.

Assessment

A quick but careful scrutiny of the victim should reveal the main injuries or problems; a full and leisurely exam can follow once this most urgent question has been answered,

Is the victim in immediate danger of dying?
Rarely in the mountains is life in imminent danger except in cases of airway block, chest injury, severe head injury, or massive bleeding. For any of these conditions, provided the situation is not patently hopeless, act before trying to identify the precise cause of trouble. In other cases there is usually sufficient time to ask the victim what happened, and to examine him thoroughly in order to assemble the facts and reach a reasoned diagnosis. Doctors and medical personnel are trained this way and other people should do the same. Some of the terms used in the following paragraphs of this section may be unclear until the relevant chapters in the book have been read.

The injured climber is most likely to die from: extensive damage to the entire body caused by a fall; inability to breathe owing to airway block or chest injury; severe head injury and the sequels of unconsciousness; profuse bleeding causing shock and heart stop.

Airway – listen for the snoring breathing of airway block. Turn the victim into the draining position, tilt the head, remove secretions, lift the jaw and insert an oral airway. Do not make a pillow for his head.

Breathing – listen for croaking stridor and look for the rise and fall of the lower chest and upper abdomen. If absent start rescue breathing.

Circulation – look for blood from an exposed wound, feel under the victim for pooled blood soaked in clothing and lying unnoticed behind the back or head. Control bleeding with steady pressure directly on the wound. In order to assess the circulation feel the pulse at the wrist or neck, and notice the speed of return of colour to the nailbed after blanching with pressure. Look at the face for the pallor of shock and the blue colour of cyanosis.

Neurological – first and most important, assess the conscious level according to the Glasgow Coma Scale. Secondly, look at the pupils for difference in size indicating bleeding inside the skull, and at the nose and ears for cerebro-spinal fluid leaking from a fracture of the base of the skull.

Bones – feel the skull, chest and pelvis with both hands for fractures, and move the limbs gently watching the victim's face for wincing due to pain. Splint fractures and reduce dislocations if possible.

Examination

Having made sure the victim is not in urgent need of life-saving attention, and if necessary having moved him to a safe place out of danger of rockfall or avalanche and with space to move around, do a thorough and leisurely examination. The scheme: Exam, Ask, Look, Feel, Listen, Move, Act, Rx (=Treat), is a rough framework for most of the chapters in this book. Pithy words and phrases in plain English are as explicit as verbose jargon; examination, observation, auscultation, palpation.

ASK

Ask a conscious person for a full story of the accident or illness and of any symptoms (the feelings of which he complains); if the victim is unconscious ask a witness. Follow a similar routine every time you ask a story and examine someone. In this way, as in a pilot's pre-flight check, nothing important will be missed. Always write down findings immediately, or details will be forgotten later. An accurate written record will assist the receiving doctor at the hospital. Whatever scheme is adopted stick to it so it becomes routine.

General questions – name, age, address, next of kin, occupation.
– chief complaint; use the person's own words to write a sequential story of the accident or illness, asking especially about pain – time of onset, nature, severity, change in character
– past illnesses and surgery, with dates
– present medication; look for a Medic-alert bracelet or medallion
– allergies; to drugs, foods, and insect stings.

Systematic history – heart: chest pain, palpitations, shortness of breath, swelling of ankles
– chest: cough and sputum, difficult breathing, wheeze or croup
– gut: pain, appetite, nausea, vomiting, indigestion, constipation or diarrhoea
– urine: frequency, pain, burning, volume and colour
– nerves: conscious level, seizures, faints, headaches, loss of power or sensation, numbness or tingling.
– motor: pain or weakness in either bones, muscles, or joints; abnormal gait and walking.

EXAM

In a sheltered area with adequate light, undress the victim so nothing is obscured by clothing. Remember there is a back as well as a front. Cold hands will make him flinch and you will learn nothing. The order in which the victim is examined and how the findings are recorded is unimportant so long as the scheme is unvarying. Start at the crown of the head and work towards the feet. When examining a paired part, for example a limb or one side of the chest, always have the opposite side exposed for comparison; slight swelling or deformity becomes obvious when compared with the normal side. Negative findings may be as important as positive ones. Perform every step of the exam even if the injury or illness appears obvious at first sight, because a secondary condition, obscured by an exigent chief complaint, may be equally significant. The victim needs reassessing frequently, at least every half hour, because much can change after the initial exam.

The following outline is a rough check-list; refer to specific chapters for more details. Examining someone requires practice and skill, but doctors were all inept medical students once. This scheme presupposes no specialized medical equipment.

General appearance – sick or well: an impression formed by instinct rather than by specific signs
– consciousness and co-operation
– demeanour: lying still, rolling around
– pain, temperature, fever
– skin colour: anaemia, pinkness of lower inner eyelid or finger-nail; cyanosis, blue colour inside lips; jaundice, yellow colour of whites of the eyes
– skin eruptions
– hands tell a whole story about the person

Head and neck – scalp: bleeding, swelling, depressions.
– eyes: vision, pupil size, redness, discharge
– ears: hearing, discharge (blood or clear fluid)
– nose: airway, bleeding, discharge
– mouth: bleeding, breath smell, teeth and gums, tongue, jaw
– throat: redness, ulceration, pus
– glands: neck, under jaw

Heart – pulse rate and regularity, blood-pressure (judged by the force of the pulse and capillary filling – observe the speed at which the nail bed returns to a pink colour after being blanched with pressure), cyanosis, heart sounds (ear to chest), peripheral circulation (warmth and colour of the fingers and toes), ankle swelling

Chest – obvious injury (bruising or fracture), breathing movements, ear to the chest for air entry and breath sounds (wheeze and fluid, crackling or bubbling)

Abdomen – look for quiet movement on breathing, scars from previous surgery, distension, swellings, inspect genitals. Feel for tenderness, resistance to the examining hand, rigidity of muscle wall, masses or swellings, hernial openings

Pelvis and perineum – stability on pressing firmly on the hips, bruising between the legs, bleeding from the urethra

Muscular – range of movement, pain, tenderness, swelling, deformity, power, tone, co-ordination, sensation, reflexes of all limbs and joints

Neurological – conscious level (Glasgow Coma Scale), pupil size and reaction to light, mental state.

2 Equipment and drugs

Before setting out on a journey to drive across the Sahara it would
be wise to check the vehicle's tool kit, and the vehicle, in order to
make sure everything is present that might be needed to deal with a
breakdown. For similar reasons information on equipment and
drugs is included at the very start of this book so the reader may
know what is available to assist him in dealing with the emergency
at hand.

The contents of the First-Aid kit (F-A) will fit in a waterproof
plastic box measuring 12 cm × 12 cm × 4 cm (5″ × 5″ × 2″); the
Medical kit (Med), which is more comprehensive, in a box 24 cm ×
16 cm × 6 cm (9″ × 6″ × 3″). On an expedition bulkier equipment
and more drugs can be carried to base camp and the contents (Base)
can be quite sophisticated, especially if a doctor is present.

Equipment

ITEM	F-A	MED	BASE
soap bar	*	*	
alcohol swabs		*	
Band-aids (assorted)	*	*	
Elastoplast strip 3″	*	*	
surgical adhesive tape: 1″	*	*	
3″		*	
Steristrips	*	*	
moleskin	*	*	
bandage: elastic 3″	*	*	
knitted cotton 3″	*	*	
triangular		*	

ITEM	F-A	MED	BASE
safety pins	*	*	
sterile gauze: plain	*	*	
non-stick		*	
wound dressing no. 15		*	
paraffin tulle graz		*	
Sofratulle	*	*	
gelatin foam		*	
scalpel blade: no. 11	*	*	
no. 15		*	
forceps: thumb		*	
tweezers: eyebrow		*	
SAK	*		
scissors: dressing		*	
SAK	*		
forceps, locking (mosquito)		*	
syringes 3 ml		*	
needles no. 25		*	
waterproof matches	*	*	
luggage label	*	*	
wax pencil	*	*	
magnifying glass	*	*	
tongue depressor		*	

ITEM	F-A	MED	BASE
penlight		*	
thermometer: regular		*	
low reading			*
flashlight			*
antiseptic concentrate			*
finger dressing, Tubegauz			*
head dressing, elastic net			*
plaster of Paris / C-Cast			*
wire mesh splints			*
tincture of benzoin			*
needle holder			*
sutures: 2/0 catgut			*
4/0 nylon			*
syringe 10 ml			*
needles, hypodermic, no. 20			*
surgical gloves			*
cervical collar			*
oral airway			*
nasopharyngeal airway			*
stethoscope			*
blood-pressure cuff			*

ITEM	F-A	MED	BASE
ophthalmoscope			*
auroscope			*
Foley catheter			*
i/v drip set			*
i/v fluids			*
cricothyroidotomy tube (sterile, wrapped)			*
dental forceps: upper			*
lower			*
dental probe			*

SAK: Swiss Army Knife

Drugs

ITEM	STRENGTH	F-A	MED	BASE
D.1 Analgesics				
D.1.1 paracetamol	500 mg tab		*	
D.1.2 naproxen	250 mg tab		*	
D.1.3 codeine	15 mg tab	*	*	
D.1.4 morphine	15 mg tab		*	
	15 mg/ml amp			*
D.1.5 naloxone	0.2 mcg/ml amp			*

ITEM	STRENGTH	F-A	MED	BASE
D.2 Antibiotics				
D.2.1 cephalosporin	250 mg tab		*	
	2 mg amp			*
D.2.2 co-trimoxazole	960 mg tab		*	
D.2.3 metronidazole	250 mg tab			*
D.3 Antihistamines				
D.3.1 promethazine	25 mg tab	*	*	
	25 mg/ml amp			*
D.3.2 chlorpheniramine	4 mg tab		*	
D.4 Steroids				
D.4.1 prednisone	5 mg tab		*	
D.4.2 dexamethasone	0.5 mg tab			*
	20 mg/ml amp			*
D.5 Sedatives				
D.5.1 lorazepam	1 mg tab		*	
D.6 Diuretics				
D.6.1 frusemide	40 mg tab	*	*	
	10 mg/ml amp			*
D.6.2 acetazolamide	250 mg tab			*
D.7 Cardio-vascular drugs				
D.7.1 glyceryl trinitrate	0.5 mg tab			*
D.7.2 adrenaline	1 mg/ml inj			*

ITEM	STRENGTH	F-A	MED	BASE
D.8 Respiratory drugs				
D.8.1 salbutamol	4 mg tab		*	
	puffer			*
D.9 Digestive system drugs				
D.9.1 aluminium hydroxide	500 mg tab		*	
D.9.2 famotidine	40 mg tab		*	
D.9.3 loperamide	2 mg tab		*	
D.9.4 bisacodyl	5 mg tab		*	
D.9.5 bismuth subgallate	200 mg suppos			*
D.10 Skin antiseptics				
D.10.1 povidone-iodine	concentrate			*
D.11 Skin applications				
D.11.1 betamethasone	0.1% oint			*
D.11.2 clotrimazole	1% cream			*
D.11.3 PABA sunscreen		*	*	
D.11.4 Calamine	oint			
D.11.5 lip salve		*	*	
D.11.6 methyl salicylate	oint			*
D.12 Eyes				
D.12.1 chloramphenicol	1% oint	*	*	

ITEM	STRENGTH	F-A	MED	BASE
D.12.2 dexamethasone	0.1% oint		*	
D.12.3 homatropine	2% drops		*	
D.12.4 Amethocaine	1% drops		*	
D.13 Ears				
D.13.1 chloramphenicol	1% oint		*	
D.14 Nose				
D.14.1 ephedrine	1% oint			*
D.15 Throat				
D.15.1 lozenges			*	
D.16 Teeth				
D.16.1 oil of cloves			*	
D.16.2 temporary filling			*	
D.17 Local anaesthetic				
D.17.1 lignocaine 2%	20 mg/ml vial		*	
D.18 Oral rehydration constituents			*	

A mythology exists about the merits of particular drugs, encouraged by the habits of the prescriber and by advertising propaganda of the drug manufacturers. Certain principles in recommending drugs are explained here; choice should be based on fact and good advice.

In the text drugs are given their scientific, generic names by which they are known world-wide. Prescribing the generic name is usually cheaper because drug companies load the cost of research and development onto their own brand names. It is also much safer because there can be no confusion over the name as it is the same in Tokyo or Timbuktu. When two drugs have similar action, the cheaper one is usually chosen; although cost is a factor in assembling a good medical kit, it should not hamstring the choice if an expensive drug is markedly preferable. Small quantities are being considered, and when they are needed only the best will do. If one drug has more than one action it is preferred. In order not to confuse a harassed rescuer one well-tried drug, or possibly two, have been selected from each treatment category rather than offering many choices; many different antihistamines are available but promethazine and chlorpheniramine have stood the test of time. Medication once or twice daily is more likely to be taken by the person in need, so is preferred to more widely spaced timing of drug-taking.

When recommending a drug, or a piece of equipment I avoid repeatedly writing 'if available'. Included in my selection are such drugs and medical material as might reasonably be included in a mountain medical kit, which should be comprehensive, compact and light. Most drugs are conveniently carried as pills or tablets rather than as liquids, which freeze, are bulky and the bottles or ampoules easily broken. However, some drugs are best injected for speed of action, control and to avoid vomiting; this book presumes that the larger medical kits may include them, or that they may be found at base camp, where they will necessarily require syringes and needles as well. The technique of intramuscular injection can be learned from any competent nurse and practised on an orange which has the form and consistence of skin. Intravenous injection requires more skill, but millions of junkies have learned how.

Drugs are chosen to cover the widest spectrum of action, for example, the antibiotics cephalosporin and co-trimoxazole cover wide antimicrobial contingencies with few side-effect complications. If the person is sensitive to one, the other should be used. Sound hospital medicine is quite different to that practised by a climber in the hills with a small medical kit and limited experience, and drugs may have to be chosen that would not be used in a more elaborate setting. Doses are given for an average-sized adult. Adjustments must be made for size and age. Children take roughly half the adult dose, infants a quarter. The possible side-effects of the drugs are spelled out. Pregnant women should beware of taking any drugs, unless well-advised.

Morphine and codeine are controlled drugs, that can only be prescribed by a registered physician under specific guidelines. When approached by climbers for small quantities of such drugs for their first-aid or medical kits, provided I know they are competent to use the drugs safely, I prescribe a small amount (30 tablets maximum), writing the name of the person followed in red ink by 'for expedition use only'. The climber is instructed that the name of the person to whom the drugs are administered, the date and the quantity must be written down each time and produced before any re-supplies will be prescribed. This seems a reasonable way to ensure that the law regarding controlled drugs is observed, although nothing specific is written concerning the dispensing of such drugs by non-medical personel, which is inevitable in a climbing situation.

Each drug (D) is given a number; the first figure refers to the category, the second to its place within that group, for example (D.1.3) means the drug is in category 1, analgesics, and is number 3, codeine. When drugs are referred to in the text they are given this number and the rescuer must refer back to this chapter for details of action, dosage and side-effects. When the choice is equal just the category number is given (D.1). Thus this chapter deserves careful study before reading the rest of the text.

The specialized drugs mentioned in the Foreign Travel section are found only there and not in this general drugs section. When a drug is recommended in the text that does not appear in the medical kit it is enclosed thus [ergometrine], for example. Certain standard abbreviations are used throughout the book.

Rx:	drug treatment
s/e:	side-effects
i/m:	intramuscular
i/v:	intravenous
s/c:	subcutaneous
s/l:	sublingual

D.I ANALGESICS

Pain is always unpleasant and often unnecessary because, with adequate dosage of analgesics, most pain can be controlled. Pain is subjective and people's stoicism and their response to analgesics, varies.

MILD ANALGESICS – *Paracetamol* will control most headache and mild muscular or skeletal pain, and reduce fever. It has advantages over aspirin in causing less irritation to the stomach and possible bleeding, and fewer sensitivity reactions. (Aspirin should be taken only in its enteric-coated form which is only released after passing through the stomach, which is thus protected from its corrosive acid effects.)

Naproxen is one of many anti-inflammatory drugs not related to steroids, which are also analgesic; it may be taken in addition to other stronger narcotic analgesics. The twice daily dose is an advantage as people are less likely to forget to take it. Naproxen is useful for inflammatory conditions like arthritis, tendonitis, and bursitis.

Compound analgesics containing aspirin or paracetamol mixed with codeine or caffeine or both, have no advantages and are expensive.

All these drugs are taken by mouth after meals.

D.I.I paracetamol
Rx: 500 mg–1 g every four to six hours to maximum 4 g daily
s/e: rare hypersensitivity and skin rashes

D.I.2 naproxen
Rx: 250–500 mg twice daily
s/e: occasional stomach upset. Use cautiously with sufferers of stomach ulcers, asthma, and aspirin sensitivity. It may cause fluid retention at altitude.

MODERATE ANALGESICS – *Codeine* is a great multi-purpose drug. It relieves moderate pain, and can be given together with paracetamol to increase the analgesic effect of the latter; it is excellent against diarrhoea and night-time coughing. Codeine is legally narcotic and potentially addictive, but dependency is uncommon. It suppresses cough, and reduces bowel motility thus slowing diarrhoea. It is the analgesic of choice in head injury because it affects pupil size and breathing less than morphine.

D.1.3 codeine phosphate

Rx: 10–60 mg by mouth four-hourly to maximum 400 mg daily
s/e: constipation, drowsiness, dizziness, alcohol enhancement.

STRONG ANALGESICS – *Morphine* is a time-honoured, strong analgesic effective against severe pain, whose action may be enhanced by the euphoria it produces. It is narcotic, causing sleepiness and is also strongly addictive. It depresses breathing and causes pin-point pupils, so should not be used when breathing is compromised, as in asthma and some chest injuries, or in head injury when it depresses breathing and alters pupil size, which is an important diagnostic sign. A well-respected mountaineering and emergency physician says,

> . . . all strong analgesics depress respiration; this effect is dose-related, as is the pain relief. Pain-killers don't 'kill' pain. They need to be given until the conscious person says, with a big grin, 'yes, it hurts like hell and I don't give a shit', not to a point of stupor.

Morphine constipates; it may cause nausea and vomiting. These side-effects can be lessened if it is combined with promethazine which does not diminish the analgesic power and may even enhance it.

Morphine tablets, placed under the tongue (or even better the more recently introduced synthetic opioid, buprenorphine), although bitter tasting, are quickly and evenly absorbed; but swallowed morphine tablets are absorbed poorly from the stomach and the drug is broken down by the liver before it reaches its site of action in the brain. Hence the sublingual route is now preferred by many pain clinics, even though morphine has traditionally been given intravenously in small doses, repeated as often as needed. When given to a shocked person the drug can lie stagnant at the site of injection because of poor circulation; when the latter picks up, a slug of the drug is released suddenly with the danger of depressing breathing. Ideally the narcotic antagonist drug naloxone should be available in order to reverse respiratory depression.

Pethidine is weaker than morphine and has no advantage so gets no space here.

D.1.4 morphine sulphate

Rx: 10–30 mg maximum, four-hourly s/l, s/c, or i/m.

By i/v Rx: 5 mg every five minutes until pain is relieved and then repeated as frequently as needed to control pain.

s/e: respiratory depression, constipation, urinary retention, nausea, tolerance and dependence. Avoid in head injury, asthma, breathing difficulty, and druggies.

D.1.5 naloxone, narcotic antagonist

Rx: 40–200 micrograms i/v, and add 40 micrograms every two minutes as needed to restore normal breathing; it can also be given i/m or s/c.

s/e: nausea and vomiting.

D.2 ANTIBIOTICS

Antibiotic drugs combat bacterial infections; virus illnesses are generally untreatable so antibiotics should be eschewed. Ideally bacteria should be grown in culture and their sensitivity ascertained before starting an appropriate antibiotic. However, in the wilderness no such scientific accuracy is possible and a blunderbuss approach is in order, using an educated guess at which broad-spectrum antibiotic will be effective.

The only logical way to choose amongst the myriad antibiotics on the market is to take sound bacteriological advice and select two or three antibiotics in order to combat the widest range of organisms, with due consideration to cost and availability. Cephalosporins have superseded amoxycillin, a broad-spectrum penicillin (which used to be the antibiotic of choice) because many organisms have become resistant to it. Five per cent of the population are penicillin-sensitive, but only ten per cent of penicillin-sensitive people are allergic to cephalosporin. Ninety per cent of Staphylococcus aureus, the universal organism of wound and soft tissue infections and burns, all of which may be commonly encountered by mountaineers, are resistant to amoxycillin whereas cephalosporin is effective against it.

Cephalosporin is the name of a group of broad-spectrum antibiotics of which there are several to choose from, all with very similar actions, for example, cefaclor, cephalexin, cephradine. Hence the group name is offered rather than any single drug, for which advice can be taken from any doctor or pharmacist. Cephalosporin is also very effective given i/v.

Cephalosporin is *bactericidal* and effective against group A streptococcus, Staphylococcus aureus, ampicillin-resistant Escherichia coli and Proteus mirabilis, Klebsiella pneumoniae, and Strep. pneumoniae, but ineffective against pseudomonas and Strep. faecalis.

Rx: infections of skin and soft tissue, the middle ear, upper and lower respiratory tract (including streptococcal sore throat), and urinary tract.

Co-trimoxazole, a mixture of five parts sulphamethoxazole and one part trimethoprim, is the other antibiotic of choice.

Co-trimoxazole is *bacteriostatic* and effective against Staph. aureus, H. influenzae, E. coli, klebsiella, enterobacter, Proteus mirabilis and vulgaris, Salmonella typhi and paratyphi, and shigella, but ineffective against Strep. faecalis and other streptococci.

Rx: infections of burns, skin and soft tissue, bone and joints, the lower respiratory tract (bronchitis and pneumonia) and urinary tract; it is useful in bacterial diarrhoea and in people who are allergic to penicillins and cephalosporins, though not if sulpha-sensitive. If a known doubly sensitive person is on a trip tetracycline or erythromycin should be taken as a substitute.

Metronidazole (Flagyl) is active against anaerobic bacteria and protozoa, but has less antibacterial value than either cephalosporin or co-trimoxazole. It is well absorbed, giving high blood-levels for a prolonged period, and, in the wilds far from help, would cope with persistent diarrhoea of Entamoeba histolytica or Giardia lamblia, and with peritonitis following a ruptured appendix.

A full course of antibiotics usually lasts five to seven days and should not be curtailed, but can be lengthened if the response is slow. For convenience antibiotics are taken by mouth, but in severe infections they are more effective i/v, though only sophisticated medical kits will carry them in this form. Do not take alcohol when on antibiotic treatment.

D.2.1 cephalosporin

Rx: 250 mg eight-hourly, doubled in severe infection

s/e: hypersensitivity and allergic symptoms of urticaria, rashes, nausea, vomiting, diarrhoea, and in rare cases, anaphylaxis.

D.2.2 co-trimoxazole

Rx: One double-strength tablet twice daily, doubled in severe infection

s/e: nausea, vomiting, rashes, and various blood disorders.

D.2.3 metronidazole

Rx: 500 mg eight-hourly

s/e: nausea, drowsiness, headache, rashes.

D.3 ANTIHISTAMINES

Antihistamines dampen allergic reactions and ease hay fever, itching, skin rashes, vertigo and motion sickness; they are mildly hypnotic. They are used i/v in the emergency treatment of severe allergic reactions but are of no value in asthma.

Promethazine is well-proven, it lasts up to twelve hours, and is quite sedating. It alleviates nausea and vomiting and can be given together with morphine, the analgesic effect of which is not diminished and may even be enhanced.

Chlorpheniramine is shorter-acting and less powerful, but is good for daytime use in treating allergies because it induces less drowsiness.

D.3.1 promethazine (Phenergan)

Rx: 25 mg by mouth eight-hourly to maximum 150 mg daily

s/e: drowsiness, headaches, urinary retention, dry mouth, blurred vision

D.3.2 chlorpheniramine (Piriton)

Rx: 4 mg by mouth eight-hourly

s/e: less sedating than other antihistamines.

D.4 STEROIDS

Prednisone has widespread effects on the body and so should be
used cautiously. It suppresses severe allergic reactions and may be
effective in severe asthma, status asthmaticus and acute
hypersensitivity reactions. In the wilds it could save the day for
someone with an acute prolapsed disc or a severe gout attack, at
least allowing them to walk to safety.

Dexamethasone may reduce the brain swelling in cerebral
oedema of high altitude, and in trauma from head injury.

People taking steroids should wear a Medic-alert bracelet or
medallion and carry a card in their wallet with instructions on how
to adjust their dose in case of emergency.

Medical-alert bracelet

D.4.1 prednisone

Rx: a short sharp course starts with 40 mg daily (2 × 5 mg tablets
six-hourly), reducing by 5 mg every day, and continuing at 5 mg
daily for a week. Courses of steroids are usually tailed off gradually,
but can be stopped abruptly if the course has lasted less than three
weeks.

s/e: steroids have many hazards, particularly in suppressing
adrenal gland function and the normal inflammatory response.
They should be taken under medical supervision.

D.4.2 dexamethasone (Decadron)

Rx: 4 mg i/m or by mouth every four to six hours, or 10 mg i/v, or
i/m.

s/e: as above.

D.5 SEDATIVES

Benzodiazepine drugs are useful hypnotics for insomnia at high altitude or for long plane flights, and as sedatives in low doses for acutely anxious persons. They will control epileptic seizures when given i/v until the person can begin specific anti-epileptic medication. Benzodiazepines differ mainly in their length of action.

Lorazepam is one of many available, being fairly quick of onset and short in action. It is less cumulative than other benzodiazepines.

Promethazine (D.3.1) is a useful mild sedative.

D.5.1 lorazepam
Rx: 1–4 mg by mouth at night, 0.5–1 mg by day
s/e: drowziness, dependency, habituation.

D.6 DIURETICS

Diuretics promote urine flow, and thus decrease oedema by suppressing reabsorption of sodium by the kidney; coincidentally they lower blood-pressure.

Frusemide is powerful and short-acting, and only the smallest dose necessary to obtain the required effect should be used, with caution; it may be used to treat oedema of high altitude, of heart failure, pulmonary oedema, and peripheral oedema of the feet, ankles, and hands. Diuresis starts within an hour and is complete in six hours, so it is best taken in the morning because frequent peeing will disturb sleep. Used over a long time frusemide causes loss of potassium, which must be replaced as potassium tablets or by fruit juice.

Acetazolamide is used to diminish the incidence and effects of acute mountain sickness.

D.6.1 frusemide (Lasix)
Rx: 40–120 mg daily by mouth, i/v not faster than 4 mg/minute
s/e: potassium loss, rashes, ringing in the ears

D.6.2 acetazolamide (Diamox)
Rx: 250 mg by mouth 1–4 times daily
s/e: numbness and tingling fingers, toes, face; dry mouth, makes beer taste foul.

D.7 CARDIO-VASCULAR DRUGS

People with heart problems usually carry their own medications; mountains are no places to be starting cardiac drugs of unpredictable action and response.

Glyceryl trinitrate dilates blood-vessels to the heart and relieves the chest pain of angina; it works within seconds and lasts less than an hour.

Adrenaline relieves acute asthma, severe allergic reactions and anaphylactic shock; it can be dangerous in older people because of causing heart irregularities.

Digoxin is risky to use and probably better left out of a medical kit.

D.7.1 glyceryl trinitrate
Rx: 0.5–1 mg under the tongue and repeat in half an hour if needed

s/e: throbbing headache, flushing, faintness

D.7.2 adrenaline
Rx: 0.5–1 mg of 1:1000 solution by subcutaneous injection every ten to fifteen minutes for three doses if needed

s/e: rapid, irregular pulse, anxiety, tremor, dry mouth, cold hands and feet.

D.8 RESPIRATORY DRUGS

Salbutamol is the safest bronchodilator drug and relaxes the tight wheezy breathing of asthma; it works rapidly when inhaled from an aerosol puffer, but is more sustained when taken by mouth. Beware of taking too much from the puffer because the drug is unevenly absorbed.

D.8.1 salbutamol (Ventolin)
Rx: 4 mg by mouth every six to eight hours; two puffs of aerosol every six to eight hours; 0.25–0.5 mg s/c or i/v in severe asthma

s/e: rapid pulse, headache, tremor.

D.9 DIGESTIVE SYSTEM DRUGS

Antacids – neutralize acid produced by the stomach and ease the discomfort of indigestion, gastritis, and the pain of peptic ulcer. They need to be taken frequently, after meals. Antacids bought in roll packets are convenient to carry in the pocket; tablets can be crushed to powder and made into a paste for greater effect. Medication should go hand in hand with eliminating fatty or spiced foods, and avoiding nicotine, alcohol and coffee, all of which encourage gastric acid secretion.

D.9.1 aluminium hydroxide
Rx: by mouth 500 mg tablets as needed

Acid-Reducing drugs – heal peptic ulcers; they block histamine receptors in the stomach, reduce gastric acid, and allow healing. They have no effect on bleeding ulcers.

D.9.2 famotidine
Rx: 40 mg by mouth once daily at bedtime
s/e: diarrhoea, skin rashes, dizziness.

Gut-slowing drugs – slowing the motility of the gut reduces diarrhoea. All narcotic drugs have this effect, often undesirable when used for pain relief.

Loperamide is poorly absorbed from the gut so remains longer where its action is needed; it can be used in parallel with codeine (D.1.3), for greatest effect. Antibiotics should generally be avoided in diarrhoea, which may be worsened because normal and necessary bowel organisms are killed as well as harmful ones.

D.9.3 loperamide (Imodium)
Rx: 2 mg eight-hourly
s/e: dry mouth, rashes

Laxatives – increased dietary roughage and fibre, like horses' bran and whole wheat, along with fruit juice, especially of prune and fig, may solve the problem more simply and safely than drugs. Motility-increasing drugs, if needed, act within six to twelve hours and are fairly gentle purgatives which stimulate gut motility.

D.9.4 bisacodyl (Dulcolax)
Rx: 5–10 mg after meals; by suppository 10 mg
s/e: abdominal cramps, diarrhoea

Piles and anal itching – helped by scrupulous toilet, washing with
soap and water after a bowel movement, avoiding constipation, and
a bland astringent soothing cream. Sometimes hydrocortisone (HC)
and local anaesthetic are incorporated into the drug.

D.9.5 bismuth subgallate (Anusol HC)
  Rx: ointment or suppository twice daily

D.10 SKIN ANTISEPTICS

Antiseptic solutions cleanse and disinfect closed skin and open
wounds, but may cause sensitivity and have no advantage over
washing with soap and plenty of water, hence are listed here only
for completeness. They are best carried as concentrate which can be
diluted with cooled boiled water.

D.10.1 povidone-iodine (Betadine)
Weakly antiseptic solutions can be made from crystals whose bright
colour may contribute to their placebo effect; brilliant green,
gentian violet, potassium permanganate, methylene blue.

D.11 SKIN APPLICATIONS

Itching (pruritis) is often less bearable than pain and can drive a
person crazy; where possible treat the cause first. Topical
antihistamines and local anaesthetics are poorly effective and may
cause skin sensitization. Oral antihistamines are useful to subdue
allergic skin rashes. Usually antiobiotic creams are best avoided
because most wounds and minor burns heal when left open to the
air to dry; nothing supplants cleaning with soap and water, and
systemic antibiotics are more effective than creams in many skin
infections.

  Calamine ointment soothes itching skin.

  Steroid creams suppress skin inflammation, especially eczema,
and relieve symptoms but do not cure the condition. Beware of a
rebound worsening effect on ceasing treatment. Side-effects may
occur with long-continued use.

  Clotrimazole is used against fungi, like monilia and tinea.

  Sunscreens with PABA filter out the burning, erythema-
producing parts of the ultraviolet spectrum.

D.11.1 betamethasone (Betnovate) 0.1% cream, strong steroid
Rx: apply thinly two to three times daily
D.11.2 clotrimazole (Canesten)
Rx: apply two to three times daily, continuing for one to two
weeks after the lesions have healed
s/e: skin irritation and sensitivity
D.11.3 para-amino benzoic (PABA) esters
Rx: apply one hour before exposure and frequently thereafter
D.11.4 calamine ointment
D.11.5 lip salve
D.11.6 methyl salicylate
Rx: massage ointment to produce soothing 'deep heat'

D.12 EYES
Chloramphenicol is a broad spectrum antibiotic both for eye and
ear, and ointment can be used in both.
   Dexamethasone is a strong steroid for the treatment of iritis.
   Homatropine, a mydriatic, dilates the pupil for about twenty-four
hours and eases reflex iris spasm pain in corneal lesions.
   Amethocaine local anaesthetic acts within seconds and lasts a
couple of hours; but it delays healing and should not be used over a
long time.
D.12.1 chloramphenicol
Rx: apply 1% ointment six-hourly
D.12.2 dexamethasone
Rx: apply 0.1% ointment six-hourly
D.12.3 homatropine
Rx: apply 2% drops twice daily
D.12.4 amethocaine
Rx: apply 1% drops as needed

D.13 EARS
Chloramphenicol ointment put in the ear melts and flows through
the canal as would drops; the same tube can be used for both ear
and eye.
D.13.1 chloramphenicol
Rx: apply 1% ointment six-hourly

D.14 NOSE
Ephedrine is a safe decongestant that takes effect within a minute
and lasts four to six hours.
D.14.1 ephedrine 1% nose drops as needed

D.15 THROAT
At high altitude the cold dry atmosphere dries the throat so
lozenges are needed in bulk.

D.16 TEETH
A lost filling could be a serious problem so have some *oil of cloves*
to line the cavity, then a temporary filling will stave off the pain.
D.16.1 oil of cloves
D.16.2 temporary filling

D.17 LOCAL ANAESTHETICS
D.17.1 lignocaine 2%

D.18 REHYDRATION SOLUTIONS
Fluid by mouth goes some way in helping redress upset body-water
balance resulting from shock, burns and dehydration (especially
from diarrhoea). Give sips of fluid sufficient to quench thirst
without causing vomiting.
  The *WHO formula* is simple to make and contains most of the
essential chemical components dissolved in a litre of boiled water.

glucose	20g =	1 ½ tsp honey, corn syrup
sodium chloride	3.5g =	½ tsp table salt
sodium bicarbonate	2.5g =	½ tsp baking soda
potassium chloride	1.5g =	¼ tsp or 2 cups of orange, apple or other fruit juice

Routes for giving medications

ORAL MEDICATIONS
Medicines can conveniently be taken by mouth in the form of
tablets or capsules. Liquids, though better absorbed than pills, are
not suitable for most mountain medical kits because of weight and

the danger of breakage and freezing. Absorption from the stomach is uneven and takes a minimum of two hours, and an adequate therapeutic blood-level may not be attained for twenty-four to forty-eight hours (especially in the case of antibiotics). Hence the onset of action is slow by mouth compared with the intramuscular (fast), subcutaneous (faster), or intravenous (fastest) routes. Oral medication is useless if the victim is unconscious, vomiting, or suffering from severe indigestion and nausea. However in the mountain situation, it is usually preferable to use pills. They are absorbed most quickly on an empty stomach, but sometimes because of acid constituents, must be taken with food. Some pills, for example morphine sulphate and glyceryl trinitrate, are absorbed well from the mucous membrane lining of the mouth, and especially under the tongue, but the taste is bitter.

INJECTION TECHNIQUES

Before giving any injection read carefully, and ideally have a companion check, the label on the ampoule or vial in order to make sure that the drug intended to be given is correct in name, strength and dilution. Scrub hands thoroughly so all manoeuvres will be as sterile as possible. If the drug is in an ampoule, cover the neck with a piece of cloth or tissue, so any glass broken cannot accidentally cut the fingers. If the drug is in a rubber-capped vial, first clean the top with an alcohol swab. Assemble syringe and needle directly from their sterile packages taking care not to contaminate either. Draw a measured dose of fluid into the syringe; then hold it vertically, needle upwards, and expel any air bubbles. An orange has similar consistence to skin and can be used for practice in order to get the feel of thrusting a needle through skin, the thought of which imbues horror in many people.

Intramuscular injection – the sites of choice are deltoid muscle over the upper outer arm, a hand's-breadth below the tip of the shoulder.
– front of the thigh, mid way in a line between hip bone (iliac crest) and knee-cap
– upper outer-quarter of the buttock.

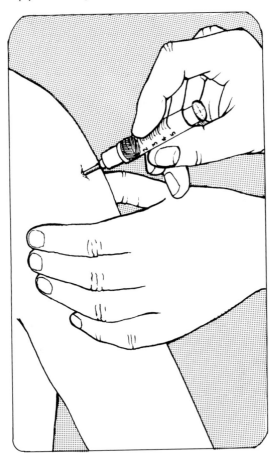

Intramuscular injection sites

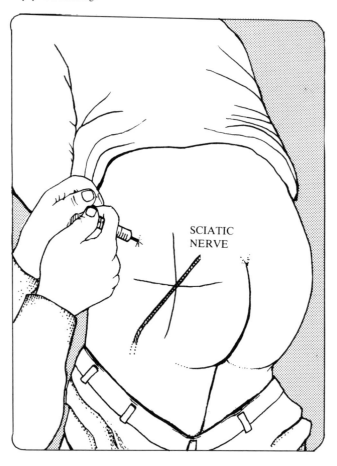

SCIATIC
NERVE

Intramuscular injection sites

Clean the skin with soap and water or an alcohol swab. Pinch the skin widely between thumb and fingers of one hand; holding the loaded syringe like a dart in the other hand, plunge it up to the hilt of the needle deep into muscle. Pull back on the plunger of the syringe to ensure the needle is not in a blood-vessel; if blood returns into the barrel of the syringe withdraw the needle and start again. Then steadily and slowly push on the syringe plunger until the contents are completely evacuated. Withdraw the needle and clean the skin with the same swab, rubbing vigorously in order to spread the injected drug in the tissues and to ease the discomfort of suddenly distending the tissues.

Subcutaneous injection – lax skin over muscle, such as the upper outer arm or abdomen, is suitable. Adrenaline is given s/c; morphine can be.

Prepare as for i/m injection above. Pinch the skin only, and insert the needle at an angle until a give is felt as the point of the needle enters the fat layer just below skin but above muscle. Pull back on the plunger and inject slowly as above.

Intravenous injection – this route is the fastest for obtaining action of the drug injected, and the technique can be learned with practice. But the effect of the drug is sudden and potent so the i/v route should only be used by someone who fully understands the action and possible complications of the drug. The technique is summarized here in order to remind doctors who have spent time away from the sharp end of practice.

Obstruct the veins of the forearm and hand, by tying some sort of tourniquet round the upper arm, in order to make the veins stand out. This can be speeded by making the person clench and open a fist repeatedly, hang an arm over the side of the bed, or immerse a hand in warm water or cover it with a hot, wet towel. Seek the largest vein on the back of the forearm for first choice, on the back of the hand next, in the crook of the elbow only if you can't find one elsewhere. Clean the skin with an alcohol swab where you intend to make the puncture. Stretch the skin over the vein tightly with one hand. Pierce the skin to the side of the engorged vein, angle the needle and advance it through the vein wall being careful not to pierce the opposite wall. Blood will return into the syringe if the needle is in place. Undo the tourniquet. Inject the required amount of drug slowly. Withdraw the needle, swab the site, and keep firm pressure for a minute. If the i/v site swells, the needle had probably punctured the vein and the drug has run into the tissues – it then has the effect of a s/c injection instead.

3   Airway block

Airway block occurs when the tongue falls against the back of the throat (pharynx), or when saliva, blood or vomit pool there; airway block can kill, so must be relieved immediately. However, any victim of severe trauma or heart attack who is not breathing is most likely dead, so only start resuscitation if there is some possibility of recovery and rescue.

Look, feel, listen

If breathing appears to have stopped bend over the person. Look for normal breathing with your eyes watching his chest and upper abdomen. Feel for breath with your cheek against his mouth. Listen with your ear against his nose. A partially blocked airway causes noisy breathing like someone snoring or croaking. The lips may be tinged blue (cyanosis) instead of their normal pink colour, and froth may appear at the mouth. If breathing is obstructed chest movement is shallow and the spaces between the ribs are drawn inwards with each breath. Breathing sounds can be heard as well with your ear placed against his chest as by using a stethoscope.

The structure and function of the tongue are crucial to understanding airway block. In quiet, normal breathing air passes through the nose; the mouth remains closed, almost completely filled by the tongue which lies well forwards against the teeth and hard palate. The tongue is fixed at its base to the lower jaw (mandible); when fully protruded only about one third of its total bulk is seen. The tongue normally stays forwards in the mouth, but while lying face upwards asleep, or unconscious, the relaxed tongue falls back by gravity against the pharynx, partly shutting off the airway. As air slips past the tongue, it vibrates against the back of the throat sounding like snoring. The tongue of an unconscious person can form an almost air-tight block, like a cork, across the pharynx.

An unconscious person may be able to vomit, but the laryngeal, cough and swallowing reflexes that prevent food, water, blood, saliva and vomit from going down the wrong way, are suppressed. If inhaled, these substances irritate the lining membrane of the terminal sacs of the lung (alveoli) causing fluid secretions, which obstruct gas exchange between blood and air.

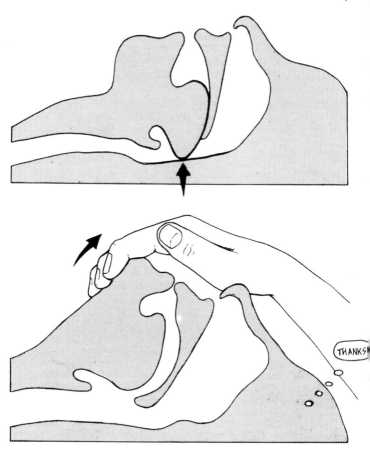

Airway and tongue anatomy

Inhaled air contains twenty per cent oxygen which, carried by haemoglobin, gives saturated arterial blood its bright-red colour, making the lips pink. After combustion in the cells some of the oxygen is converted to carbon dioxide. Exhaled air contains only sixteen per cent oxygen, venous blood is unsaturated, and so the lips may be cyanosed and bluish.

After four minutes without oxygen the brain suffers irreparable damage. More brain cells die the longer oxygen is lacking, and they cannot regenerate as cells in some organs do. Although the victim may partly recover consciousness later, his brain will be permanently damaged.

Act: if breathing is obstructed unblock the airway with utmost speed. Turn the victim into the draining position, tilt the head, remove secretions, lift the jaw, insert a plastic airway and fix the tongue. Hope he will not need an endotracheal tube, a cricothyrotomy or a tracheotomy.

Draining position: turn the victim on one side with his head lying lower than his body. Tilt the head slightly backwards (provided the neck is not injured) in order to straighten the neck and to avoid kinking the windpipe (trachea). Thus the tongue falls forward by gravity from the back of the pharynx so fluid can drain from the upper airway. This position has many names; coma, recovery, tonsil, but a single aim – drainage. If fluid has been inhaled through the vocal cords (larynx) into the lung, drainage has little effect and the victim may drown in his own juices.

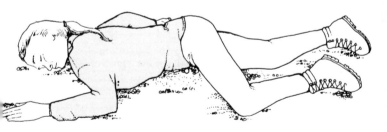

Draining position

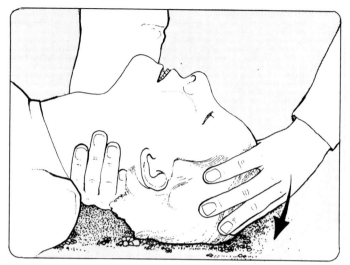

Head tilt

Head tilt: tilting the head back slightly will straighten out the trachea, which may be kinked if the neck is flexed with the chin on the chest. One hand supports the neck, the other presses down on the forehead. Even if the neck is injured it is more important to prevent the victim dying from suffocation than worrying about worsening a damaged neck, serious though that may be.

Finger sweep: put a finger, wrapped in a piece of cloth, into his mouth and scoop out any obstructing solid matter such as vomited food, blood clot, or avalanche powder-snow. Don't remove well-fitting dentures. If the victim is conscious the teeth and jaws may be clenched tight; they should not be pried open because of the risk of breaking teeth. If he is conscious he can maintain his own airway anyway. The crossed-finger manoeuvre helps to hold the jaw open gently with a single hand, provided there is not much resistance.

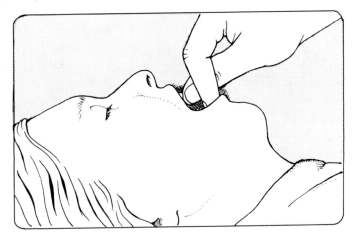

Crossed finger manoeuvre

Suck out: to remove fluid or secretions from the airway pass a flexible tube far back in the throat, suck on it and spit out the material. If secretions have pooled near the larynx this unpleasant task may be life-saving. Foot-operated suction pumps should be carried by rescue teams.

Jaw lift: lift the lower jaw, to which the tongue is fixed at its base, forwards so the tongue moves with it and cannot fall back against the pharynx with the tongue still lying back. It is easier to lift the jaw forward with the victim lying on his back, but the technique must be learned in the draining position.

With three fingers of each hand widely spaced, grasp his jaw with the little finger curled behind the angle. Push it skywards rather than merely closing the upper and lower teeth together. This position is tiring but can be held for longer if the elbows are resting on the ground. Holding the jaw with only one hand frees the other hand, but requires practice and some skill.

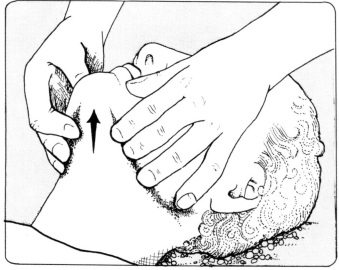

Jaw lift

Mechanical airways: insert an airway if breathing remains obstructed notwithstanding all the above. A mechanical airway is not needed by a person who resists it, gags on it or fights it, because the victim will be conscious enough to safeguard his own airway.

Oral airway: carry a small, light, cheap plastic oral airway in a first-aid kit. The shaped end curves over the back of the tongue keeping open the space at the back of the pharynx. To insert the airway open the mouth wide and pull the tongue forwards. Insert the airway, moistened in order to slide more easily, with the curve pointing towards the roof of the mouth; then rotate it over the back of the tongue. The metal tooth-guard prevents a half-conscious person biting it closed, and the flange stops it slipping down the throat.

A two-ended oral airway makes mouth-to-mouth resuscitation less distasteful. An airway with a one-way valve and a cheek-guard is more efficient and can be attached to a self-inflating bag.

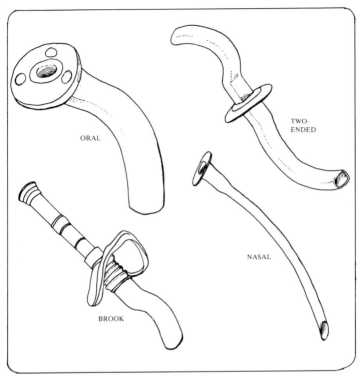

ORAL

TWO-
ENDED

NASAL

BROOK

Mechanical airways

Tongue fix: if the chin and tongue of an unconscious victim persistently fall back, (for example, while being carried on a stretcher), and if you have no mechanical airway, thrust a safety-pin through the tip of the tongue, tie a piece of string to it, pull it firmly forwards and attach it to his belt; this apparently brutal action guarantees a clear airway. Should the victim regain consciousness the pin can be removed quickly leaving minimal damage.

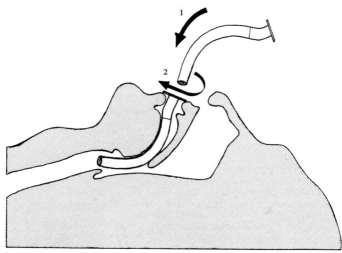

Inserting oral airway

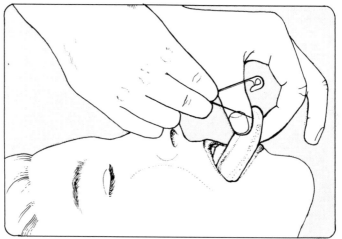

Tongue fix

NASO-PHARYNGEAL AIRWAY

Pass a well-greased tube about 15 cm long through one nostril; gently and skilfully thread it backwards until the rubber flange lies against the nose (to prevent it being sucked down into the lung). In this position the end lies in the pharynx providing a clear airway past the tongue.

CRICOTHYROIDOTOMY

A person about to die from unrelieved airway block can be saved by this manoeuvre. Needless to say, such bold surgery requires courage, skill, and good judgement. It is an acceptable procedure in dire emergencies, in the right hands.

Push a wide-bore no. 14 gauge needle (or a knife blade in skilled hands) directly into the trachea through the cricothyroid membrane which is easily found 1 cm (½") below the prominence of the larynx (Adam's apple) in the mid-line of the neck and above the cricoid cartilage. The thyroid gland and other vital neck structures are well lateral to the cricothyroid membrane, and the posterior ring of the cricoid cartilage should protect the oesophagus behind. A hiss of air is released as the needle enters the trachea. A few puffs of air (or better, oxygen) may be enough to aerate the lungs and relax spasm of the vocal cords.

The knife blade is inserted transversely through the skin over the cricothyroid membrane. The wound is spread with a knife handle or a dilator which lies in the trachea. A soft cuffed tube inserted through the hole can be left in place for two weeks or more. Pre-packed, sterile, diposable cricothyroidotomy tubes can be bought commercially.

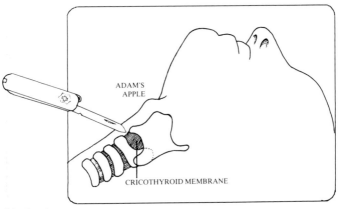

ADAM'S APPLE

CRICOTHYROID MEMBRANE

Cricothyrotomy

ENDOTRACHEAL TUBE

The technique of passing an endotracheal tube can be life-saving but should never be done by an untrained person. Forcing a tube clumsily into the larynx causes spasm of the vocal cords, which may only relax just before the victim is about to die. Endotracheal intubation is a skill that, once learned, is never forgotten; rescue-team members should ask the anaesthetist of the local hospital to teach them how.

The tube is passed through the vocal cords, using a laryngoscope, and lies in the trachea. It guarantees an open airway in all positions of the head and neck during evacuation, and the modern soft, cuffed tubes can be left in place for seven to ten days before a formal tracheotomy need be done. When the cuff surrounding the tube is inflated it seals off the trachea and ensures nothing is inhaled into the lungs. It aerates the lungs efficiently when attached to a self-inflating resuscitation bag, preferably connected to a supply of oxygen.

Tracheotomy is a surgical operation and should only be done in the operating room.

Absent breathing

RESCUE BREATHING

If the victim is unable to breathe despite an open airway, blow oxygen into the lungs urgently – but only if there is a reasonable chance of recovery and rescue.

Mouth-to-mouth – the rescuer's own nasty expired breath, although not as good as pure air, still contains sixteen per cent oxygen, enough to change the victim's colour from blue to pink. Turn him on his back, which is an easier position to do mouth-to-mouth than lying on his side. Tilt the head. Wipe away debris and secretions in his mouth. Place your mouth over his mouth and exhale fully into his mouth while pinching his nose to stop air escaping. Watch his chest, which will rise if the lungs are being adequately inflated; about ¼–½ litre of air should be shifted with each breath. Then remove your mouth and the elasticity of his own lungs will expel the air. One breath every four to six seconds is ample. If his mouth is injured breathe into his nose instead, holding his lips closed the while.

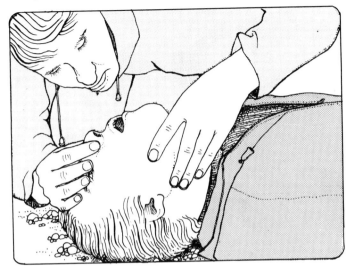

Mouth-to-mouth

SELF-EXPANDING HAND-INFLATED BELLOWS
Air is sucked through a valve at one end and expelled at the other.
Inflation is easier work than mouth-to-mouth breathing and can be
continued for longer. The bellows can either be attached to a face mask
over the nose and mouth, or be connected to a mechanical airway. If the
victim does not start breathing on his own after half an hour the rescuer
should stop resuscitation unless expert help is expected imminently.

Choking

When choking from airway block caused by a foreign body, the
victim grasps his throat, goes blue in the face and cannot speak.

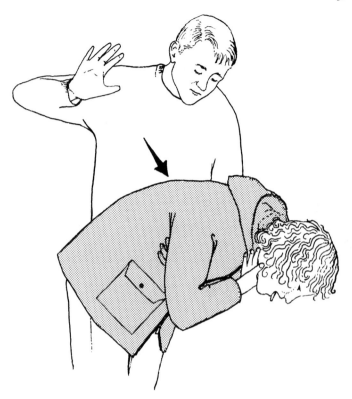

Back blows

Act: *strike four sharp blows* rapidly with the heel of the hand in between his shoulder blades while supporting his breastbone (sternum) with your other hand. Open his mouth with one hand. Grasp his jaw and pull it forward. Sweep the index finger of your other hand as far back in the throat as possible and hook out any foreign material.

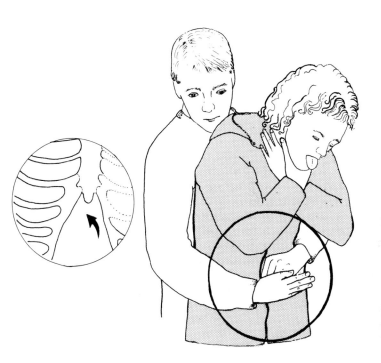

Heimlich manoeuvre

Abdominal (or chest) thrusts (Heimlich manoeuvre). Stand behind the victim, wrap your arms around him and grasp with one hand the closed fist of your other hand placed over the upper abdomen or lower chest. Give four thrusts strong enough to force air out of the lungs and to dislodge the obstruction, but not so violent as to rupture an internal organ.

4 Heart stop (cardiac arrest)

The commonest cause of heart stop, even in the mountains, is heart
attack (myocardial infarction); the heart can also stop after severe
trauma, near-drowning, a lightning strike, or deep hypothermia. In
a remote area heart stop caused by trauma is usually fatal. A
summary of cardio-pulmonary resuscitation (CPR) is given here
because it is one of the skills expected of all first-aiders, but the
chance of it being successful in the mountains is nearly zero. For this
reason I am tempted to banish this section to the end of the book
and print it small, but fear of an outcry from enthusiastic 'hands-on'
rescuers has persuaded me reluctantly to leave it in place.

Look, feel, listen

Absent pulse or heart sounds – feel the carotid pulse in the victim's
neck by sliding your fingertips into the groove between his
wind-pipe (trachea) and the neck muscles at the level of the Adam's
apple (larynx). Listen with your ear pressed against the front of his
chest to the left side of the breastbone (sternum); the heart sounds
like a distant 'lub-dup, lub-dup, lub-dup'.

Feeling the radial pulse at the wrist is notoriously misleading; the
rescuer's cold fingers searching for it under tight anorak cuffs may
get the false impression that the heart has stopped. Alternatively
feel in the groin for the femoral pulse, found halfway between the
pubic bone and the wing of the pelvis (iliac crest).

Unconsciousness – the victim looks deathly pale and does not
respond to command or pain. His pupils slowly dilate and do not
constrict to the stimulus of light.

Absent breathing – place your ear near his mouth. Listen and feel
for movement of air.

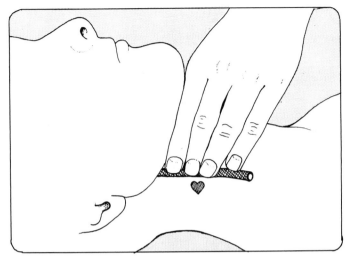

Carotid-artery Pulse

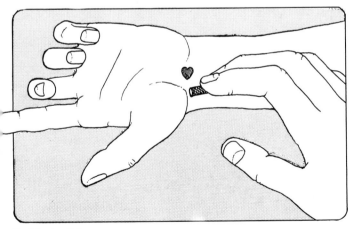

Radial-artery Pulse

Act: irreversible brain damage occurs after the heart and breathing have stopped for four minutes so CPR must be started immediately to have any chance of success. If the victim is cold and appears dead always try to resuscitate and re-warm him because he may be suffering from hypothermia instead.

Rescue breathing: start mouth-to-mouth rescue breathing immediately with four quick, full breaths, not allowing the lungs to deflate fully between breaths. One sharp blow with the clenched fist on the middle of the sternum may sometimes restart the heart; if not, begin chest compression without ado.

Chest compression: lay the victim horizontal, or slightly head down, but never head up, on a hard, flat surface in order to get the best gravity feed for blood to the brain. Later raise his feet on a rucksack to encourage venous blood to return to the central circulation. Kneel beside him, feel the edge of his rib cage, and run your fingers upwards until they meet the notch where ribs and sternum join in the middle of the lower chest. Place the heel of the other hand two finger-breadths above the notch with your fingers pointing across the long axis of the sternum. Place your free hand on top of the hand on the sternum so the fingers of both hands are parallel; fingers can be extended or interlocked, but they should not rest on the chest.

Lock your elbows straight and with shoulders positioned over your hands. Press down on the heels of your hands vertically, smoothly, and with sufficient force to depress the sternum 4–5 cm in order to squeeze the heart enough to pump blood to the brain. Some ribs may fracture but this is not serious and can be dealt with later. Release the pressure completely after each compression in order to allow the heart to refill, but do not lose contact with the sternum. Compress the chest regularly and evenly.

– single rescuer: 15:2 sequence. Compress the chest fifteen times. Then give two quick, full rescue breaths lasting four to five seconds without allowing him time to exhale fully between breaths. Feel the carotid pulse occasionally to check that heart compression is being effective, and to see if the heart has restarted on its own.

– two rescuers: 5:1 sequence. Compress the chest sixty times per minute while an assistant does rescue breathing, giving a swift

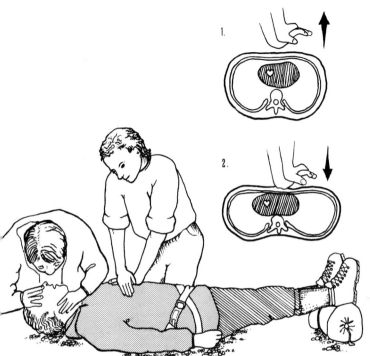

Chest compression

breath at the up-stroke of every fifth compression without
interrupting compressions. Team-work and good timing are
essential and need practice.

Once started continue CPR until spontaneous heartbeat and
breathing have returned: the victim becomes warmer; blue lips,
pale skin and mucous membranes change to pink; large dilated
pupils return to normal – continue to watch him closely because he
may relapse and need more CPR. CPR is very hard work and half
an hour is about the longest most people can manage on their own.
If the heart has not restarted within this time it probably never will.

5 Head injury

A climber may injure his head during a fall, or be struck by falling rock or ice. Hard hats, like motor cycle crash-helmets and car seat-belts, reduce the numbers of serious head injuries. Sensible climbers use them.

Generally speaking, victims with bad head injuries tend to get worse and die, not-so-bad head injuries tend to get better. Less than one per cent of head injuries need surgery; those that do, need it at once. Do not be tempted to interfere and possibly worsen things. A Swiss Army knife, an ice screw, or the pick of an ice-axe, wielded in the field by a surgeon could be life-saving; in unskilled hands they would probably be lethal weapons.

Prevent the victim from dying of, or being harmed by, other causes, the most important of which are further rock-fall and ice-avalanche, airway block, neck injury, and bleeding.

Airway block (see page 47)

Snoring, rattling breathing is a sign of a blocked airway, not of a head injury. Turn the victim on his side in the draining position, with the head slightly downhill. Don't leave him lying on his back for fear of worsening a neck injury, because his tongue will sink backwards by gravity, block the airway and kill him. Also vomit or blood from an associated face or nose injury may trickle down the back of the throat and be inhaled. Hold the jaw forward and insert an oral airway.

If the victim is deeply unconscious, or if his face is badly smashed, simply holding the jaw will probably not keep the airway open.

Insert a naso-pharyngeal tube which has the advantage of by-passing an injured mouth. This difficult procedure can be done without direct vision. If the mouth is unharmed pass an endotracheal tube using a laryngoscope. If neither method is possible a cricothyroidotomy may be necessary to prevent suffocation.

Neck injury

A victim of a head injury may also have injured his neck. Examine him carefully, avoid unnecessary movement, put on a cervical collar and strap him to an improvised spinal board.

Bleeding

The scalp and face bleed profusely and alarmingly but such bleeding is a poor indication of the gravity of a head injury.

SCALP

Wash and clean with plenty of water and, if necessary, cut away some hair in order to get a better view and gain access to the scalp. Press firmly over the wound with a dressing pad – any cotton material placed on top of a sterile gauze square usually suffices to stop bleeding. Do not remove the first blood-soaked dressing because the fresh clot will be disturbed, just add more dressings on top as required. Usually scalp wounds heal well without suturing. For an open skull wound or a suspected depressed fracture, make a doughnut dressing or a ring pad, that presses around the wound edge on undamaged skull while leaving the centre without pressure.

TEMPORAL ARTERY LACERATION

A minor cut over the temple area can sever the temporal artery which runs close under the skin over the skull and can be felt 2 cm above and in front of the pinna of the ear. Sometimes the cut end can be seen spurting and can be seized with forceps and tied; otherwise pressure will have to suffice.

FACE

Face wounds heal well but they demand accurate apposition of the edges in order to get the best scar, so use steristrips or butterflies to hold the edges together. A plastic surgeon can tidy up the scar later.

When the face is badly smashed, with lacerations around the mouth, a fractured jaw, and dislodged teeth, the airway is threatened and must be safe-guarded with an artificial airway, or better still with an endotracheal tube.

The victim of head injury may be conscious, in which case he can answer questions which will help make a diagnosis; or unconscious, when he will need to be cared for completely.

The unconscious person

After dealing with the immediately life-threatening conditions above, attend to the following:

Restless behaviour: may result from brain disturbance, pain or a full bladder. The victim may need restraining.

Pain: Rx codeine (D.1.3). Do not use morphine, which depresses breathing, alters consciousness, and constricts the pupils thereby disguising a vital observation.

Bladder: a bursting bladder causes an unconscious person to thrash about in bed. Encourage him to pee by stroking the inside of the thighs accompanied by the sound of water flowing from one cup to another.

If this fails do a suprapubic stab with a wide-bore needle (see page 130). Repeated stabs when the bladder is full is safer and less likely to result in infection than attempting catheterization in unclean conditions.

Feeding: if neglected over several days an unconscious person may become severely starved and dehydrated. He will be unable to feed himself.

Pass a naso-gastric tube with a funnel attached, by which he can be fed directly into the stomach. Plain water is better than nothing. Desist if there is any suspicion of basal skull fracture as the tube may penetrate through the fracture into the brain.

Eyes: lubricate with any eye ointment to prevent the cornea developing ulcers from exposure and drying by the air.

Skin: turn him two-hourly to prevent bedsores which readily become infected causing blood poisoning (septicaemia), a common cause of death in head injuries. Scrupulous attention to the bowels and to hygiene of the perineum will prevent soiling by faeces, which causes the skin to become raw and liable to pressure sores.

MECHANISM OF HEAD INJURY

Brain is composed of semi-solid nerve tissue suspended in cerebro-spinal fluid (CSF) which cushions movement of the brain within the skull – a rigid, protective box. CSF circulates between a layer of tissue (arachnoid), which covers the brain, and another which lies against the skull (dura). Blood-vessels lying in the space between brain and arachnoid, and between skull and dura, are liable to be torn in a severe head injury. Spilled blood has no means of escape and gathers in spaces between the covering layers causing pressure to rise inside the skull.

Primary brain injury, caused at the moment of impact by displacement, distortion and stretching of brain within the skull, dictates the final outcome of the head injury.

Skull fracture may be linear, comminuted into small fragments, depressed below the surrounding skull or through the base of the skull. The fracture is superimposed on the primary brain injury and is irreversible and may be closed or open (compound). When open, the brain communicates with the outside either directly, or via the nose or ears, when CSF leakage can be seen as drops of clear fluid. Infection can enter and the consequences may be lethal. A sulpha antibiotic is preferred, otherwise Rx: co-trimoxazole (D.2.2).

TYPES OF BRAIN DAMAGE

Concussion: a trivial blow on the head causes the brain to swirl round, nerve pathways are deranged and the victim falls unconscious briefly. After resting he may recover quickly and completely. Someone 'knocked-out' in this way may be unconscious from a few seconds up to several minutes. The speed at which he regains normal consciousness is a good indicator of the severity of the injury and of the final outcome. He may forget the impact itself, but he will probably remember events up to the accident. Then follows a measurable period of forgetfulness (post-traumatic amnesia) which is important because an injured climber may feel fine and set off alone, without recollection of the accident or of his whereabouts. He may lose his way, or worse, relapse on the way down and collapse owing to pressure from slow, hidden bleeding gathering within the skull. Anyone who has lost consciousness from a head injury, for however short a time, should not be allowed to descend unattended, even if he considers his injury trivial.

Contusion, laceration, and local damage: with more severe trauma specific areas of the brain may be bruised or mangled. The brain has well-defined areas that control limb movement, speech, and sensation. The right half of the brain controls the left side of the body and vice-versa. Local damage may cause irritation of the brain with fits of twitching of the opposite limbs; these may spread into general 'grand mal' epileptic seizures, during which the victim may die from airway block. Occasionally the limbs are paralysed on the opposite side of the body. Recovery is slow.

Clot compression: concussion may follow a trifling knock on the head or severe intracranial bleeding. The victim improves and appears quite normal a short while later (lucid interval) and he may even continue climbing. Continued bleeding (extradural haemorrhage), or swelling of the brain itself, causes pressure within the rigid skull to rise with subsequent compression of the brain. He complains of headache, relapses, and becomes more drowsy. Then he slips into coma.

The victim will die unless the blood under pressure is released quickly by a surgeon drilling a trephine hole in the skull. Brain damage from compression is permanent because cells of the outer layer of the brain (cortex) die, unlike cells in other parts of the body which can regenerate.

Rx: dexamethasone (D.4.2) may reduce the pressure somewhat. Surgery is the best treatment, so rescuers must evacuate the victim quickly.

Severe, diffuse injury: The climber is deeply unconscious from the time of injury and unable to keep an open airway. He may be lax or stiff. Unless prevented, he may roll about in a purposeless manner and fall again. If the airway is protected he may recover slowly over several months.

Observe and record

After taking immediate steps to prevent the victim of head injury dying, the biggest contribution to the final outcome will be accurate hourly recording of changing trends in his level of consciousness and his clinical progress. These notes may help the surgeon, who will see him for the first time some hours later, to decide whether to operate immediately in order to relieve pressure from bleeding within the skull (cerebral compression). If observations are not written down *during* the tumult of the rescue, they won't be remembered accurately enough afterwards to be of value.

ASK

In addition to the usual history ask these specific questions from the
victim if conscious, or if not, from a witness.
– details of the accident: exact time, length of fall, falling objects?
roped? helmeted?
– unconscious, if so, for how long?
– convulsions?
– alteration in victim's behaviour or level of consciousness?
– hypothermia at the site of the accident?

Look, feel, listen

Unconsciousness may be the result of convulsions, before or after
the injury, caused by illness unrelated to the head injury. Look for a
Medic-alert bracelet or neck-chain medallion which may tell of
known illnesses (epilepsy, diabetes) and current medication.

The head – remove any climbing helmet or hat in order to inspect
the whole head. Slip a hand under the neck to see if blood has
pooled there. Clean wounds with soap and water and remove blood
clot and hair in order to display the depths of the wound. Look for a
fracture, or pieces of foreign material that must be removed before
dressing the wound. Never probe a wound and risk introducing
infection, or even penetrating the brain through an open skull
fracture. A large, boggy swelling under the scalp or the absence of
an open wound suggests blood collecting at the site of a skull
fracture.

Clear fluid oozing or dripping from the nose or ears (rhinorrhoea
or otorrhoea) suggests leakage of cerebro-spinal fluid from a
fracture of the base of the skull. Bleeding from the nose or ears,
when not caused by obvious external injury, may also come from
inside the skull. Both are signs of grave injury and need urgent
surgical attention.

Rx: antibiotics (D.2) in maximum doses.

THE GLASGOW COMA SCALE

Eye opening (E)	
spontaneous	4
to command	3
to pain	2
nil	1

Best Motor response (M)	
obeys command	6
localizes pain	5
withdraws from pain	4
abnormal flexion (to pain)	3
extensor response (to pain)	2
nil	1

Best Verbal response (V)	
oriented and converses	5
disoriented and converses	4
inappropriate words	3
incomprehensible	2
nil	1

Levels of response (E + M + V)
  total 7–8: will probably survive
  total 6: doubtful outcome
  total 4–5: will almost certainly die
  total 3: nearly dead

Conscious level – the Glasgow Coma Scale is used internationally to estimate the conscious level and replaces vague, confusing terms of yore such as 'stupor' and 'black-out'. Noting the scale readings over several hours will show if the conscious level is becoming lighter and approaching normal, or is deepening because of increasing pressure on the brain from within the skull owing to bleeding or swelling.

Eyes – the pupil of an unconscious person, whose brain is being compressed by an enlarging pool of blood, dilates on the side of the clot and tells the surgeon on which side to drill a trephine hole. The pupil fails to respond by constricting to light because the occulomotor nerve, which controls pupil size, becomes stretched and eventually paralysed. If the pressure is not relieved the opposite pupil becomes paralysed and fails to constrict to light. Two fixed dilated pupils indicate the victim is almost surely dead.

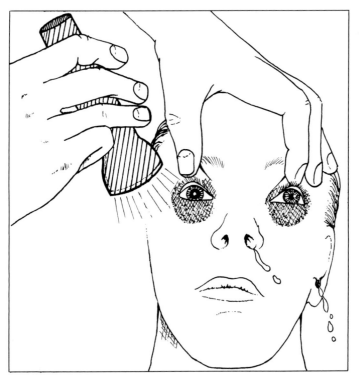

Head injury

If one pupil is bigger than the other in an awake, alert person it may be because the light is coming more strongly from one side, the pupil may have been like that since birth, or as the result of a blow on the eye (traumatic mydriasis).

If the victim blinks when a hand is waved close in front of his eye, a visual threat, the visual pathways to the brain are intact. A wisp of cotton wool touching the cornea should elicit a reflex blink.

OPHTHALMOSCOPE EXAMINATION
Papilloedema occurs in advanced cranial pressure. Retinal haemorrhages suggest the presence of blood in the sub-arachnoid space owing to sudden increase in intra-cranial pressure from the primary brain injury.

Pulse, breathing, and temperature – raised pressure inside the skull causes the pulse to slow and blood-pressure to rise, as opposed to shock in which the pulse quickens and blood-pressure falls. Breathing becomes irregular and periodic (Cheyne-Stokes). The temperature of the victim of a severe head injury may soar to 41°C (106°F) or more because of a disturbed heat-regulating centre. Cool him vigorously with cold water, ice, or snow.

Sensation and power – loss of feeling to light touch with a pin, or numbness and tingling may indicate damage to the peripheral nerves, spine, or brain. Progressive one-sided weakness suggests localized brain damage. The limbs may become partially or completely paralysed.

Consider other causes of coma in an unconscious person who tells no story, nor shows any sign of head injury. Look for a Medic-alert bracelet or medallion. But remember that the victim may also have struck his head while falling unconscious for other reasons.

6   Spinal injury

All head injury victims with altered consciousness, as well as those people complaining of neck pain after injury, should be treated as having a fracture or dislocation of the spine until proved otherwise: fifteen per cent will have such injuries. Care of the airway is paramount so gently moving the neck, for instance head tilting and jaw lifting, is in order. First-aiders are often brain-washed against moving under any circumstance the victim with a neck injury, resulting in life-threatening injuries being inadequately treated. Airway block kills people far more often than the neck injury itself.

Neck fracture and/or dislocation

Suspect a fracture and/or dislocation if the victim has been, or still is, unconscious; fell from a height and injured his head or face (twenty per cent have associated spinal injury); complains of neck pain and tenderness, or holds his neck in an abnormal position; complains of loss of feeling, or tingling and numbness, in the hands or arms; is uncooperative and mentally changed, resulting from head injury, shock or even alcohol.

Act: take the victim with all speed, but without further damage, to a hospital where he can be X-rayed, accurately diagnosed and given expert treatment. In the meantime do the best you can and make sure he does not die from causes other than the neck injury. If the spine is fractured and/or dislocated the injury will probably be so severe you are unlikely to worsen the damage; the paraspinal muscles go into rigid spasm splinting the neck, so any subsequent displacement will be minimal compared to the initial force which caused the injury. However, bruising and swelling may spread upwards in the spinal cord progressively affecting higher levels.

If the victim is awake and alert and wants to move his neck let him do so; the main reason for splinting the neck is so the rescuers cannot unwittingly upset an unstable fracture and/or dislocation making it worse. Similarly, if he wants to and can walk, let him do so. If he cannot move himself he may have to be moved to a safer place to be resuscitated or splinted to a spinal board.

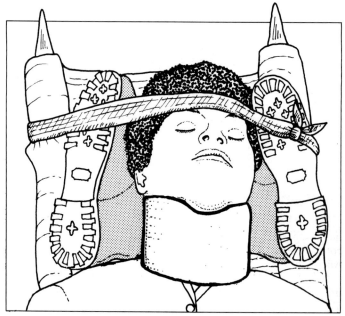

Neck injury – collar and head strap

Splinting: make a collar of tightly-rolled clothing or newspaper, aluminium foil, or a well-padded wire splint about 10 cm wide, and secure it around his neck with tape so it fits snugly under his chin. Do not try to correct any deformity of his neck. Splint it with two rolls of clothing on either side of his head, or with a pair of boots, soles outwards uppers under the neck. Strap, or tape, round the forehead so the head is splinted to the spinal board (see below).

Moving: before moving the victim give a strong pain-killer. Move him in one piece to avoid increasing the displacement of any dislocated vertebrae. One rescuer holds the head, one the legs and another the body; all move together on command so the victim's

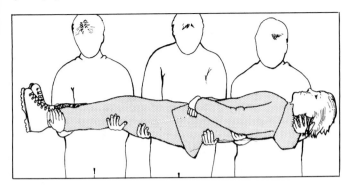

One piece move

head does not twist on his shoulders, nor his body on his pelvis. A
collar alone will not entirely stabilize the neck, but a spinal board
will do so.

Spinal board: lay him flat on a spinal board which can be
improvised from two pack frames lashed together, or on a stretcher.
Tie him so firmly to the board that he cannot move and yet the
board can be tipped over in case of vomiting.

AIRWAY
Naso-tracheal intubation is preferable if the victim is breathing; if not, do
a cricothyrotomy. A naso-gastric tube reduces the chance of vomiting and
aspiration and it prevents distension of the stomach from gastro-intestinal
ileus which often accompanies spinal injury.

Rx: codeine (D.1.3). Avoid narcotic drugs like morphine which
depress breathing and could kill someone whose chest muscles are
paralysed.

dexamethasone (D.4.2) may decrease spinal cord swelling.

Back injury

A severe back injury, though unlikely to kill someone outright, may paralyse from the waist down. A paralysed person may be surprisingly tranquil; he feels as though he is cut in half with no feeling below the waist. At the site of injury he will feel pain, which radiates round his middle from that level and shoots down his legs. If he can move fingers and toes, and can feel light touch, no nerves are damaged. But do not move the limbs actively or you may cause further injury.

Act: if he is *conscious*, in full control of his airway, and can walk by himself, let him do so. If he cannot walk he will probably be most comfortable lying on his back on a stretcher.

If he is *unconscious* tie him firmly to a spinal board or stretcher which can be tipped on its side should he vomit. Loosen tight clothing. Pad bony prominences, between the knees and ankles, and body hollows, especially behind the neck. Bandage his legs together so he may be more easily moved in one piece.

If he is *paralysed*, turn him every hour. A paralysed person cannot feel pain or the normal sensations of touch, pressure and temperature. He will lie quite still and pressure on the skin, normally relieved by shifting body position, will hamper blood-flow locally causing painless sores which can develop in less than an hour and take weeks to heal, especially if infected. Make sure he is not lying on crumpled bedding or clothing. Remove from his pockets hard objects, which cause uneven pressure. If incontinent of bladder or bowels keep him clean and dry with regular hygiene and, if possible, an indwelling catheter.

MECHANISM OF SPINAL INJURY
The spine's twenty-four vertebrae form a column between skull and pelvis. Forces are transmitted through bony vertebral bodies, behind which lie vertebral arches that form a protective tunnel for the spinal cord. Nerves to the arms leave the spinal cord highest, then those for the trunk, and finally those for the legs. The spine can bend and twist by way of many vertebral joints. Semi-solid discs between the vertebrae act as washers to cushion stress forces. Ligaments and powerful muscles stabilize the entire length of column.

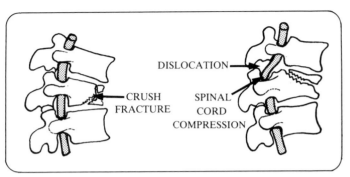

Vertebral fracture

A fractured or dislocated vertebra may damage nerves by pressure and sheering. The higher the spinal cord injury the more extensive will be the damage to nerve pathways below that level. If the cord is cut across in the neck, all four limbs, chest and abdomen will be paralysed (quadriplegia); if the injury is in the middle of the back only the legs and bladder will be affected (paraplegia). Damage to the brain paralyses the opposite side of the body because nerve pathways cross in the brain stem (hemiplegia).

Other spinal problems

WRY NECK (acute torticollis)
The neck and head are pulled towards one shoulder because neck muscles go into tight spasm, usually on waking after sleeping in an awkward position.
   Act: apply ice packs alternating with heat and gentle massage.

NECK SPRAIN (whiplash)
Whiplash can occur after a fall without visible damage to either head or neck. Severe neck pain may last several months.
   Rx: analgesics (D.1), cervical collar.

BACK STRAIN (lumbago)

The paraspinal muscles go into painful spasm in order to splint the vertebral joints.

Rx: analgesics (D.1), rest, local heat and avoid heavy lifting or bending.

SLIPPED DISC (sciatica)

A prolapsed intervertebral disc may press on spinal nerve roots causing pain and tingling along their distribution: the arms if a cervical vertebra, the legs if lumbar. Sciatica is pain felt in the leg along the course of the sciatic nerve; in the buttock, down the back of the thigh, into the calf and possibly as far as the heel or foot. Pain may be accompanied by loss of sensation and weakness. The straight leg can only be raised 30°–40° from the horizontal.

Rx: analgesics (D.1), rest on a firm surface, evacuate if signs of nerve pressure are present.

prednisone (D.4.1) in a desperate situation only it might allow a person to walk out to safety.

PERIPHERAL NERVE INJURIES

Most will return to normal once the offending stimulus is removed.

Lateral femoral cutaneous nerve – a tight waist belt may cause loss of feeling in the upper outer thigh.

Brachial plexus palsy – roping down and tight pack-sack shoulder straps cause pressure on the brachial plexus. The whole arm may go numb and feel weak. If the upper spinal cord only is affected sensation is lost over the tip of the shoulder, the upper outer-arm and the forearm. The elbow cannot be moved outwards nor can the hand rotate.

Anterior tibial compartment, 'shin splints' – over-use causes pain in the muscle lateral to the ridge on the shin bone (tibia). The foot cannot be flexed upwards and so drops and drags on walking, which can be permanent. Sensation is diminished in a small area on adjacent sides of the big toe and second toe.

This can be a surgical emergency, and fasciotomy is needed to avoid foot drop.

7   Chest injury

In a serious mountain accident both head and chest may be injured, but the chest injury may pass unnoticed because it is less obvious. However both head and chest must be examined because injuries to either may be fatal, the chest often more rapidly so than the head.

The chest may be crushed (closed injury) by a tumble onto rock, a falling stone, or by sudden tightening of a climbing rope or harness after a fall. It may be punctured (open injury) by a spike of rock or the pick of an ice-axe.

Act: immediately, before attempting a diagnosis. Keep the airway open; seal the open wound with a thick, impermeable dressing like paraffin gauze, plastic kitchen wrap or a plastic bag taped to the skin all round, in order to prevent escape or entry of air; splint the chest by binding the victim's arms, bent at the elbow, across his chest.

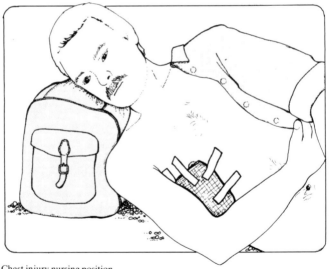

Chest injury nursing position

Turn him so he lies on the injured side with the weight of his own body splinting the chest wall which may be unstable. Use clothes as extra padding and to add pressure.

> If the airway remains blocked and if cyanosis persists despite the above, consider endotracheal intubation or cricothyrotomy and artificial ventilation.

Rx: morphine (D.1.4) may be needed to control pain and allow deep breathing. Traditionally narcotics are not used in chest injury because they depress respiration; but by relieving pain most people with chest injury breathe better, so be judiciously bold. Morphine can always be reversed with naloxone (D.1.5).

antibiotic (D.2.1 or 2.2) if spit is green or yellow, (always ask victim to spit into a tissue and look at the colour) or if there is fever.

local anaesthetic (D.17), injected directly into a rib fracture relieves pain for twenty-four hours, but beware of slipping the needle between the ribs and puncturing the lung.

Deep breathing exercises improve aeration of the lungs. In order to clear secretions encourage coughing by holding the lower chest for support. Steam can be inhaled from a pot of boiling water in order to liquefy junk in the chest and to make spit easier to cough up. Do not splint the chest with strapping or bandages as they diminish breathing movement and encourage pneumonia.

MECHANISM OF CHEST INJURY

The chest is a bony cage that acts like a bellows; it expands as the ribs move upwards and outwards, and the diaphragm moves downwards like a piston. Quiet breathing, done by the diaphragm alone, is seen as a gentle rise and fall of the upper abdomen with just a little movement of the chest. Deep or laboured breathing uses the intercostal muscles between the ribs and accessory muscles in the neck. The lungs are suspended inside the chest cavity, which together with the lung surface is covered by pleura, a membrane allowing the two surfaces to slide over each other without friction. The lung is normally held expanded against the chest wall by a vacuum in the pleural space which, if destroyed, causes the lung to collapse (pneumothorax). The air passages branch like a tree; trachea, bronchi, bronchioles and alveoli, the terminal air sacs.

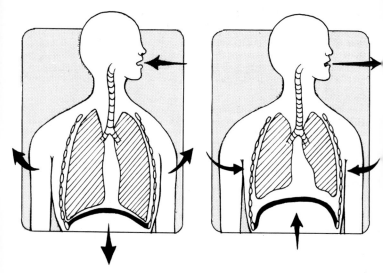

Mechanics of breathing

Look, feel, listen

Look at the victim in good light. He may show few signs of injury; his colour will be difficult to see if he is unwashed and weather-beaten or if seen inside a coloured tent. Open his clothing to display the whole chest, not just inside the top shirt button. Bluish lips (cyanosis) indicate inadequately oxygenated blood. Shock pales the face and accentuates cyanosis, present anyway in most climbers above 4,000 m (13,000 ft). Blood-flecked spittle suggests lung oedema. A skin wound or bruising of the chest points to the injured side. After injury breathing is shallow, irregular, and rapid (more than thirty breaths per minute), and the chest moves less on the injured side. Breathing and coughing are painful. When breathing is severely stressed the nostrils flare, neck muscles are taut, and intercostal muscles are indrawn.

Feel the rib cage gently for tenderness, and for an unstable segment of chest wall. Place your palms flat on the sides of his bare chest; they should move apart equally with each breath. Crackling of air bubbles in the tissues (surgical emphysema) feels like paper being rustled.

Listen for the croaking sound of obstructed breathing, and for a hiss of air escaping from a chest wound or the sucking noise of air entering.

Chest wall injury

SIMPLE RIB FRACTURES

Fractured ribs are usually caused by a direct blow. The resulting bruise can hide a litre of blood. Ribs can fracture spontaneously after a violent bout of coughing at high altitude. Severe pain, especially on breathing, comes from broken rib-ends grating against sensitive overlying periosteum. Tenderness is felt over the point of fracture. Fractured ribs heal on their own in three to four weeks but remain painful during most of that time, especially on deep breathing. Pain leads to shallow breathing and discourages coughing so secretions accumulate and become infected. Long-acting local anaesthetic injected directly into the fracture site can relieve pain for up to 12 hours. Yellow or green spit, perhaps with blood, indicates pneumonia, the dreaded complication of chest injury.

MULTIPLE RIB FRACTURES

When several ribs are fractured and the chest wall is pushed in, jagged rib-ends may puncture the underlying lung releasing air into the pleura (pneumothorax), or tear the intercostal vessels causing blood to pool in the chest (haemothorax). It is impossible to differentiate between these two in the outdoors; you may notice the lung on one side is collapsed, but telling which side is not easy (see below).

Fractures of ribs 9, 10, and 11 on the left side may damage the spleen, on the right side the liver. If the pleural lining of the chest wall is breached air may leak into the tissues (surgical emphysema) and creep up into the neck where bubbles are felt crackling under the skin.

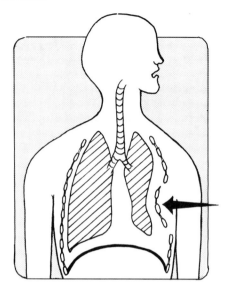

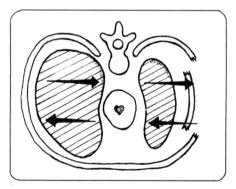

Flail chest

FLAIL CHEST

If several ribs are broken in two places, a segment of chest wall is isolated like an island and moves in the opposite direction to the rest of the chest during breathing. It is sucked in on inspiration when the chest normally expands, and is blown out on expiration when the chest deflates (paradoxical breathing). All the effort of breathing is spent in moving the unsupported flail segment rather than shifting air into and out of the lungs, which become poorly ventilated causing the victim to become cyanosed and go blue from lack of oxygen. Extra effort to breathe increases the paradoxical movement making the situation worse. He becomes anxious, restless and sweaty.

Act: mild paradoxical breathing may need no treatment. If severe enough to cause distress, fix the mobile segment of chest wall by pressing on it. The victim will immediately breathe more easily and become pink again. Tape a wound dressing over the injured ribs and turn him on that side in order to splint the broken ribs under the weight of his own body and prevent the segment of chest wall moving in and out.

> If this fails endotracheal intubation or cricothyrotomy and artificial ventilation may be necessary along with rapid evacuation to a hospital.

Lung injury

PNEUMOTHORAX OR HAEMOTHORAX

Air or blood can enter the pleural space either from outside by way of a penetrating wound; or from within due to an alveolus ruptured by a fractured rib; or spontaneously in a healthy young person. The vacuum in the pleural space is then destroyed so the lung, or part of it, collapses. Air sealed in the chest may be absorbed slowly and the lung will re-expand. If not, air may have to be drawn off through a needle.

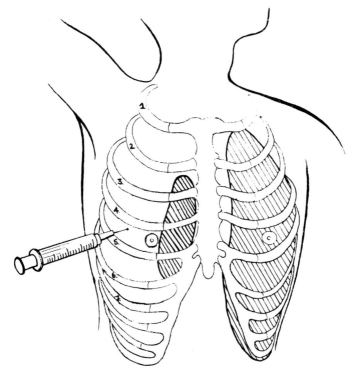

Pneumothorax, needling

To decide which lung is collapsed may be very difficult even with a stethoscope; it is vital to be sure because needling the one good lung might collapse it. With the victim breathing through his mouth listen carefully for breath sounds, which will be decreased or absent on the affected side. If breathing becomes restricted by a collapsed lung and the victim looks as if he will die, decompress the chest with a needle.

Act: push a wide-bore needle between the ribs at or above the level of the nipple in a line vertically below the mid-point of the axilla, between the folds that make the armpit. Point the needle upwards and backwards to where a chest tube would be placed if such were practicable. Allow a hiss of air to escape as he breathes out, then seal the needle with a finger when he breathes in. When all the air appears to have escaped, or blood has been sucked off, pull out the needle and cover the hole with tape. A simple one-way valve can be made by tying a condom tightly onto the needle and cutting off the rubber tip. Decompression may have to be repeated if the chest fills up again. Underwater seal drainage is preferable for continuous decompression in hospital.

TENSION PNEUMOTHORAX
Urgent, on-the-spot, definitive action is needed, because tension pneumothorax kills fast, especially at altitude. If a lung wound does not seal on its own, a flap of tissue may act as a one-way valve; air is sucked in with each breath but the flap-valve is closed on expiration. This can cause pressure on the mediastinum (trachea, heart and great vessels) and obstruct return of blood to the heart, and also its output. Air can be removed with a needle as described above. A simple pneumothorax will not kill but a tension pneumothorax may.

8   Shock

Shock is a vague term describing how the body reacts to life under threat when the effective circulating blood volume is suddenly reduced. Shock may be caused by severe haemorrhage, major burns, profuse vomiting and diarrhoea, overwhelming infection, acute pain or emotion and heart failure.

In haemorrhagic shock a chain reaction unfolds. Bleeding reduces the volume of blood returning to the heart, which consequently pumps less blood into the circulation. The fall in blood-pressure is sensed by receptors in the carotid arteries which cause the heart to speed up and to push out more blood in an attempt to keep the brain and vital organs adequately oxygenated. In order to pool blood in the centre of the body blood-vessels in the extremities of the limbs and the gut clamp down; the skin is by-passed and turns cold, pale and waxy-blue, like death.

If shock is not reversed the victim becomes breathless, thirsty, and sick; finally he is restless and confused. Unless blood-pressure is restored to normal by blood transfusion or intravenous fluids the victim will fall unconscious and may die. Prolonged low blood-pressure causes irreversible changes in kidneys, adrenals, heart and brain. He may die even if blood is replaced, if it is left too late.

Once severe bleeding is staunched write a record of the victim's progress as a means of assessing whether he is improving or worsening. With hidden bleeding these observations may be the only guide to his condition.

Symptoms and signs

Rapid, feeble pulse over 120 per minute. The force of the pulse against the examining fingers is only a rough guide to blood-pressure, it requires a sphygmomanometer for accurate measurement.

Pale, cold, clammy, bluish skin normal skin is pink and warm.

Capillary blood flow the big toe-nail or thumb-nail blanches when squeezed, the normal pink colour returning instantly on release of pressure. The speed of return is a good indicator of general blood-pressure. Delay of several seconds, with cold hands and feet, and a cold nose suggests shock or dehydration.

Restless behaviour especially true of children in shock.

Thirst unquenchable.

Dry, furred tongue usually becomes moist again after two or three days when the ability to eat and drink returns. Encourage drinking fruit juice to restore lost potassium.

Low urine output collect and measure all urine over a twelve-hour period, in dehydration it is dark and concentrated, pale and dilute normally. He should pass more than 25 ml of urine each hour, indicating that fluid intake is adequate.

Sluggish gut movement shock can paralyse the intestines and the victim may vomit. His gut does not absorb water adequately and his belly may become distended (paralytic ileus).

VISIBLE BLOOD-LOSS

Estimating blood-loss in soaked garments is often misleading but it indicates roughly the gravity of the injury and how much blood needs replacing. An egg-cupful of blood on a white shirt looks like an ocean to a lay observer, who is more likely to exaggerate than to underestimate blood-loss. An injury may appear minor on the front of the victim but a litre or more may have soaked into the clothing and sleeping bag he is lying on.

INVISIBLE BLOOD-LOSS

In closed wounds blood spreads along tissue planes causing swelling, or into body cavities displacing and irritating the contents. The available space dictates the direction and pressure of the swelling. A fractured femur can bleed a litre into the thigh making it swell to twice normal girth; the swelling may extend up to the hip and down to the knee.

   Act: *Fluid replacement:* If the victim feels thirsty give sips of water, enough to quench thirst without making him vomit. After bleeding, body-water is drawn into the blood by osmotic pressure in order to compensate for lost plasma. Although not as good as replacing blood intravenously, fluid by mouth goes some way in helping to redress the upset body-water balance.

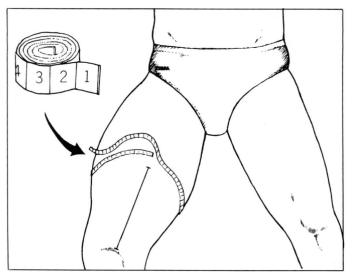

Blood-loss in fractured femur

The best composition for oral rehydration would be the WHO formula (D.18).

Blood lost should be replaced, ideally with blood but this is rarely possible outside hospital. Other intravenous fluids (normal saline or Ringer's lactate), if brought by the rescuers, should be started before evacuating the victim in order to swell his plasma volume and alleviate shock. An intravenous drip provides a route for administering drugs in finely controlled doses.

Position: keep the victim's body tilted head down, so blood will flow by gravity to the brain and prevent shock and loss of consciousness. With head wounds keep the head up.

Raise the feet above the level of the heart by placing them on a rucksack. About 2 litres of blood, pooled in the legs, is thereby returned to the central circulation. Elevate the wounded part because gravity lowers the pressure in arteries and veins locally and allows clotting.

Rest, reassure, and relieve pain: rest slows the heart while exercise speeds it. Resting the injured part encourages clotting and prevents a delicate web of early clot being broken or dislodged. Having dressed, packed and bandaged the wound, splint it like a fracture and leave it undisturbed.

Reassure the victim that bleeding is under control because, humane considerations apart, anxiety quickens the pulse and raises the blood-pressure.

Pain makes a person restless even if he is unconscious. Half-measures are useless; severe pain in a fit adult should be treated with full doses of morphine (D.1.4), provided there is no breathing difficulty or head injury, when codeine (D.1.3) is the drug of choice. Most chest injury victims breathe better when their pain is relieved. As well as easing pain, these drugs give a pleasant feeling of warmth and well-being.

Warmth is akin to comfort. Clothe the victim and shelter him from the elements. He will probably feel cold because of some degree of shock.

Appearance of other sorts of bleeding

Climbers are most likely to encounter bleeding from wounds, but they should be aware of other sorts of bleeding and the varied appearance of spilled blood. For more detail on the conditions mentioned here refer to appropriate chapters later in the book.

SALIVA

A nosebleed, bitten tongue, bleeding gums or tooth socket, injury to the nose, mouth or pharynx may cause bright-red blood to trickle into the throat. It may be spat out mixed with saliva either as streaks or lumps of clot, or it may be swallowed. Look carefully with a strong light for the source of bleeding. One very serious cause may be a fracture of the base of the skull, when blood may also come from the ears, but in both cases it is mixed with watery cerebro-spinal fluid.

SPUTUM

Pink flecks coughed up in frothy phlegm suggest blood from the lungs, possibly due to pneumonia, pulmonary oedema or embolus (fluid or clot in the lungs).

VOMIT

Swallowed blood irritates the stomach causing vomiting. If blood has lain for more than a day in the stomach it becomes partly digested and changes colour from bright red to dark brown like coffee grounds. Having excluded the causes above, a bleeding peptic ulcer is most likely.

URINE

Scanty blood turns the urine cloudy or slightly orange; if profuse, a deep wine-red colour. If peeing causes burning pain look for infection. When the story tells of a blow in the loin, suspect bleeding from the kidney. If pain is acute in onset, colicky and extremely severe, a stone in the urinary passages is possible.

STOOL

A little bright-red blood streaked on the toilet paper suggests a crack at the anal margin caused by a small pile (haemorrhoid), or by passing a constipated stool. Piles can bleed alarmingly, with clots. Digested blood (from an ulcer) that has passed the length of the gut produces, six to eight hours later, a dark or tarry stool which can be confused with the black stool of someone taking iron tablets.

VAGINA

Normal menstrual rhythms are often interrupted by an energetic pattern of living, particularly on climbing trips. The history of a missed period suggests pregnancy, so consider the diagnosis of a miscarriage (abortion) or a ruptured ectopic pregnancy in someone with vaginal bleeding.

9 Limb injury

Soft tissue injuries

Injury to muscles, tendons and ligaments are common in the mountains but their importance far exceeds their severity because they hamper the escape of an injured climber to the relative safety of the valleys.

BRUISES AND CONTUSIONS

Muscle haematoma – a muscle blood-vessel broken by a blunt blow, for example in the thigh or buttock, can leak a litre of blood into surrounding soft tissues. This forms a tense, painful swelling (haematoma) which may take weeks to subside.

Act: if the swelling has a soft centre plunge a wide-bore needle into it after carefully cleaning the skin. If you strike gold, a fluid of that colour will flow out. This is serum from broken down blood cells.

Subperiosteal haematoma – a blow on a bone near the skin surface, for example on the front of the shin, may cause bleeding under the periosteum, the thin membrane that enwraps bone and under which run nerves and blood-vessels. The pooled blood-bruise lifts up the periosteum, stretching it and causing much pain and tenderness. But the volume of blood that collects is less than in loose muscle tissue because the tension that builds also compresses the bleeding vessels. So subperiosteal haematomas rarely need to be drained.

Act: rest, elevation and ice quell further bleeding and reduce swelling.

SPRAINS AND STRAINS

Ligaments and muscles may be stretched or torn when a joint is bent beyond its normal range of movement, yet the bones remain intact. A sprain swells immediately, usually round a joint; it hurts and is very tender. A sprain is not deformed, which distinguishes it from a displaced fracture or a dislocation. If the joint can be stressed by bending it past its normal limits, a ligament tear is likely.

A severe sprain is as crippling as a fracture, and can take as long, or longer, to heal. Ankles, knees and thumbs are commonly sprained by climbers and skiers.

Act: cool with ice or snow for 15 minutes in each hour, or bathe in a stream to reduce swelling and relieve pain. Rest the elevated limb above the level of the body in order to reduce bleeding and swelling. Support the joint firmly with tape, or elastic bandage.

TEARS
Commonly torn are knee and ankle ligaments, Achilles and biceps tendons, and knee cartilages.

Act: immobilize tears by splinting, surgical correction can follow later.

TENDONITIS, BURSITIS, ARTHRITIS
Inflammation of a tendon, bursa (a fluid-filled cushion beneath a tendon) or a joint is painful and incapacitating because the underlying joint becomes stiff. Examples are shoulder (subacromial bursitis), elbow (epicondylitis), hip (trochanteric bursitis) and heel (Achilles tendonitis).

Act: rest, elevate, ice.

Rx: paracetamol (D.1.1) relieves pain and naproxen (D.1.2) reduces inflammation.

VEINS
Rupture, from blunt injury will cause a big haematoma (eg long saphenous vein). Inflammation causes thrombo-phlebitis.

Superficial thrombo-phlebitis – the vein becomes tender, hardened into a cord and the overlying skin turns red (eg varicose veins of the leg; forearm veins after i/v injection).

Deep thrombo-phlebitis – deep veins of the legs can become inflamed and clot (thrombosis) particularly if a climber lies around storm-bound at altitude and if he does not drink enough. The blood then becomes viscous, treacly and liable to clot forming a pulmonary embolus – a very serious matter (see below). Pain arises deep in the calf; feet and ankles swell. Pushing on the ball of the foot to bring the big toe nearer the kneecap causes pain deep in the calf (Homan's sign). The temperature is raised.

Act: rest with legs elevated and bandaged from groin to ankle until at least three days after all pain has subsided. Then evacuate urgently.

Pulmonary embolus – when a clot from a deep-vein thrombosis in the calf detaches, the resulting embolus travels to, and through the heart, coming to rest in the lungs. A big clot can kill owing to massive right heart failure; in a less severe case the victim is shocked, breathless and cyanosed. Sudden pain in the chest may be confused with heart attack. Cough produces blood-stained, often frothy, sputum. Deep breathing hurts.

Cerebral embolus – causes a stroke; one side of the face or the body becomes weak or paralysed.

Bony injuries

JOINT DISLOCATION

Dislocation occurs when one bone in a joint is displaced. The signs are similar to a fracture – swelling, deformity, pain, loss of use – but the diagnosis is usually obvious from the abnormal position of the joint compared with its uninjured opposite.

Act: attempt to reduce a dislocation in the same way as a fracture. If done immediately it may be quite easy, but after a few minutes the muscles overlying the joint go into tight spasm and nothing short of a general anaesthetic will relax them. Nerves and blood-vessels lie close to joints so always feel for pulses before trying to reduce a dislocation. Surrounding ligaments and soft tissues may be torn. Do not be deterred from having the courage to try to reduce a dislocation that may help a crippled climber become one who can help himself and others to retreat safely.

Rx: morphine (D.1.4); then pull firmly and steadily (traction) in the axis of the limb with an assistant giving counter-traction in the opposite direction, before attempting any specific manoeuvre to reduce the dislocation (see specific dislocations, page 102).

FRACTURE

To fracture is to break, no more no less, but a fractured femur sounds more scientific than a broken thigh. Just as a chair-leg will break if you knock, bend, twist, pull or crush it beyond a certain limit, so will bones break or crack. The difference is that wood is inert but bone is a plastic, living framework wrapped in a tough membrane of periosteum to which muscles, tendons and ligaments are attached. Periosteum is rich in nerve fibres and registers most of the pain of a broken bone. Bones mend in the same way as wounds heal.

The distinction between closed and open fractures is important in practical care. A closed fracture has the overlying skin intact, this is breached in an open fracture. Whether skin is broken from within by jagged bone-ends, or by force from outside, the underlying fractured bone is open to infection, which delays healing, smoulders and may progress to deep infection of bone (osteomyelitis) – a dreaded complication.

All fractures need splinting to prevent the broken fragments moving against each other and causing pain and further damage to neighbouring muscles, nerves and blood-vessels. Stable fractures, which are immobile, may become unstable if inadequately supported.

Look, feel, listen

Ask: how the accident happened, whether the victim heard the crack of breaking bone, where he feels pain and whether he can move the part himself.

Look at the injury. Remove clothing, if necessary by cutting along seams, in order to inspect the injury. Always compare the injured side with its uninjured normal opposite; slight swelling or deformity become obvious at a glance.

Feel the limb, beginning away from the area of pain and gradually working towards it. Keep watching the victim's face. Nothing will be learned from staring at your examining hands, whereas even a flicker of pain will register on his face. Hurting a person is inexcusable and many medical students have failed their final exams for doing so.

Shock – The victim may be shocked because of severe pain or anxiety about the outcome of his accident; a forced bivouac or a rescue call-out. He may also be in physiological shock from loss of blood into the tissues causing a lowered blood volume with low blood-pressure and rapid pulse. A severely fractured femur may cause a litre of blood to collect in soft tissues around the bone (ie 1/5 of the total blood volume). Bleeding comes from the bone marrow cavity, vessels in the periosteum and surrounding muscle, and tissues torn by the jagged bone-ends. With multiple fractures and open wounds the blood-loss may be fatal.

Symptoms and signs

Pain – most fractures cause a dull ache; when the bone fragments move suddenly causing the ends to grate, or the periosteum to stretch, they become excruciatingly painful. Tenderness is invariable and gentle pressure over even a small break causes pain, which worsens shock.

Swelling – hidden bleeding and oedema fluid cause swelling, which can be reduced by rest, elevation and ice. Bruising appears later as blood seeps through to the skin.

Open wounds needs special care before splinting in order to avoid infection. Clear away dirt and debris, and wash the wound with soap and plenty of water; cover with a bulky sterile dressing held firmly in place with tape.

Rx: broad-spectrum antibiotic (D.2) and tetanus toxoid as soon as possible.

Deformity – correcting a severe angular deformity early, before swelling and muscle spasm develop, is safe and harmless provided it can be done without undue resistance from, or pain to, the victim. Go ahead,

– if you have the expertise and confidence to do so, knowing it will take many days to reach help;

– if the bone is markedly mal-aligned and in peril of stretching or pinching nerves or blood-vessels (check for the return of an absent pulse after straightening);

– if the skin is taut and blanched, suggesting the blood supply is compromised by pressure from within.

Loss of use – the victim will hold the part quite still, guarding it from pain. Let him do so, this is Nature's splinting. Loss of use is a strong indication of fracture, because pain and instability discourage movement.

Associated damage – damage to soft tissues around the fracture may be worse than to the bone injury itself.
– blood-vessels: tear and bleed. Pinching an artery in the fracture, or spasm resulting from irritation by a broken bone, restricts the circulation to the whole limb. Tissues around a fracture swell and hamper blood-flow.
– skin: is weakened by swelling, stretching and bruising. If it breaks, a closed fracture becomes an open one. Blood-flow is usually adequate if the skin beyond the injury is warm and pink. Beware if skin goes blue or white, remains blanched on pressure and if the pulse is absent.
– nerves: may be damaged causing numbness, loss of pain and sensation, and paralysis.
   Act: if the climber is only severely bruised or suffering a sprain he may, after firm taping, be able to continue unaided. If a leg is fractured he will have to be carried or assisted, with the delay and danger that entails.

   With a suspected fracture loosen tight clothing and avoid bandages which restrict circulation. Splinting is the key to managing fractures because once an unstable bone is immobilized, the victim can be handled with less pain and further damage is avoided. Complete immobilization is possible only in a plaster cast.

Reducing – before trying to reduce a fracture reassure the victim and quietly explain what you intend to do so he will be as relaxed as possible and not surprised by sudden movement.
   Rx: morphine (D.1.4); a nip of brandy will relax the victim, but alcohol is not a pain-killer.
   Exert traction, best done with two people pulling in opposite

directions. Take a firm grasp on uninjured skin well away from the fracture and gently pull on the limb for three to five minutes to overcome muscle spasm; a helper holds the limb near the trunk, giving counter-traction. Handle the limb in one piece so the bone-ends do not grate. Sudden painful movement will cause the overlying muscles to lock firmly in spasm and any chance of reducing the fracture, especially in a muscular victim, will be slight. Traction usually removes pain; if it persists keep pulling before attempting to reduce the fracture. It also improves circulation and nerve function across the fracture site.

Reduce the fracture by increasing traction gently, firmly, resolutely and without hurry. Watch the victim's face all the time. Once the bone-ends are separated pain is relieved and it is easier to restore them to their natural position ready for splinting. But do not relax traction until the limb is splinted. Do not persist in hurting the victim by seeking perfect alignment. Aim to get the bone roughly straight, an orthopaedic surgeon can tidy up any angulation problems later.

Splinting – splint a fracture so the joints above and below the break are immobile. Splinting may be delayed if being trussed up in an awkward situation on a mountain means the victim cannot help in his own evacuation to a safer place. If he has to be carried on a stretcherpad below weight-bearing points (eg heels) and between bony prominences (eg ankles) using spare clothing or a ring pad like a doughnut. Fill the hollows under the knees. Tie splinting bandages firmly but not so tight as to impede the circulation. Leave toes and fingers open to view so their colour and temperature can be observed; undo the whole splint and bandage if they become pale, blue or cold. With swelling a tight splint can quickly become a tourniquet. Climbing leaders and wilderness guides should practice making splints before a trip. When improvising a splint in earnest, try it on the uninjured limb first.
– body splints: the most available splint is the body itself. A broken arm can be splinted to the chest and a broken leg to the opposite uninjured leg with padding inbetween.

– improvised splints: imagination designs improvised splints; surgical tape will secure them in place.

Arm: closed cell foam pad (cut to size); bark peeled from birch, poplar, alder or any hardwood; newspaper or a magazine rolled into a tube; cardboard cut and shaped to an angled gutter.

Leg: tree branch or ice-axe; tent pole, ice picket, ski, telescopic ski-pole, canoe paddle.

Ankle: down jacket, clothing.

Back: two pack-frames strapped together; a cabin door or a ladder; two paddles.

Crutch: trim a stout sapling at a Y-junction.

– malleable splints: Kramer wire; wire mesh ¼″. Bend to conform to the shape needed.

– inflatable splints (often carried by rescue teams): the limb is put into an inflatable double-skinned tube, different sizes for arms and legs. Leg splints wrap around the limb and are closed by a zip-fastener or Velcro self-adhesive material. Put an arm splint over your own arm, wrist end first. Grasp the victim's hand, as in greeting, and slide the splint from your arm onto his. Inflatable splints can be blown up too tight and cut off blood supply; no harm will come if they are inflated by mouth so they can still be easily indented with finger pressure. They must be let down every two hours and re-inflated. Always leave the fingers and toes open for inspection of colour and temperature. Inflatable splints fold away neatly and can be put on over clothing. With careful handling they should not puncture. If evacuating the person by air, splints must be partially deflated because of pressure change at altitude.

– plaster splints: fibreglass (C-cast) should replace plaster-of-paris for mountain rescue use; it is light, waterproof and durable, though expensive. It makes a rigid cast that can be moulded to the limb. A back slab is the safest plaster splint for an arm or leg. The cast is moulded onto the natural contour of the back of the limb, encasing not more than three-quarters of the circumference so the remaining gap allows the limb to expand if it swells. The limb is then wrapped in a light bandage, shirt, or under-clothes and the plaster is put on over it. The limb should be on slight traction in the normal position at rest. Don't aim at perfect position as the cast can be replaced on reaching hospital.

Never apply plaster directly to the skin; put it on over padding, either of wool or the victim's clothing left in place. Fold any loose ends back so there is no chance of them rubbing the skin when the plaster hardens. Wear a pair of large disposable surgical gloves to apply the plaster; they should be packed with the rolls in the medical kit.
– traction splints: useful for lower limb fractures. The Thomas splint (see page 112) has been used for over a century. It is still useful for mountain rescue teams but too bulky and heavy to be carried even by a small climbing expedition. In order to give the same effect a traction device can be improvised from two pack-frames lashed together, or two ski-poles.

Specific injuries

The common bony injuries in climbing accidents are to the spine, pelvis, ribs, collar-bone, forearm, hand, lower leg and ankle. For convenience, specific injuries will be dealt with region by region.

UPPER LIMB
Injuries around the shoulder, collar-bone (clavicle), upper arm (humerus), elbow, or forearm (radius and ulna) can be immobilized with a sling and swathe to bind the limb to the chest. The weight of the arm itself gives some traction for upper arm injuries. A forearm sling is easily made with a triangular bandage or a collar-and-cuff. The sleeve of the victim's jacket can be pinned to his opposite shoulder. A swathe of rope or clothing, padded for comfort, binds and splints the injured arm to the chest.

CLAVICLE
Fractured clavicle: the clavicle lies close under the skin so any break in normal contour is easily seen.

Act: a forearm sling and swathe is preferable for a day or two, but if pain persists a figure-of-eight bandage will brace the shoulders back and prevent the broken bone-ends grating. Leave the jacket on and make two well-padded rings, one for each shoulder, out of bandage or a scarf. Use a third tie to windlass the rings together and

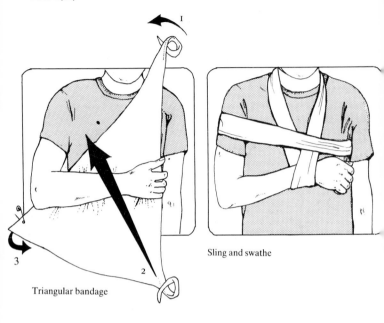

Triangular bandage

Sling and swathe

pull the shoulders back; pad between this cross-piece and the spine. If the hands tingle or go numb, slacken the windlass.

Acromio-clavicular joint separation: the tip of the shoulder is very tender and hurts if moved. A high step in the contour is obvious.

Act: a sling makes the joint comfortable until it heals, but accurate reduction is unnecessary unless very widely separated, when a surgeon is needed.

SHOULDER

Shoulder dislocation: a fairly common and dramatic injury. The head of the humerus, forming the upper arm, slips below the shallow socket (glenoid) of the shoulder blade (scapula) in which it lies. A climber, disabled and in pain can, with prompt attention, be

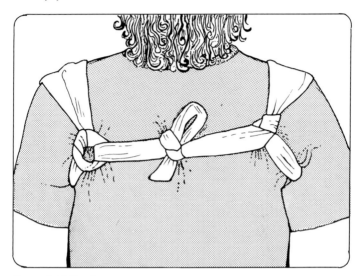

Figure-of-eight bandage

enabled to assist in his own evacuation. Every first-aider should learn how to reduce and replace a shoulder dislocation because it is one of the few medical emergencies where swift, skilful intervention by a layman can make a significant difference to the outcome, and it is so satisfying to victim and rescuer alike. Hence the space devoted here to the procedure.

A first-time dislocation, usually from a fall on an outstretched hand, needs to be reduced within minutes or else the powerful muscles around the shoulder go into spasm and lock tight because of pain. Recurrent dislocation of the shoulder affects some people, but the shoulder is easily replaced, often under the instruction of the victim himself.

Look: the rounded contour of the shoulder is lost (compared with the normal side) and the shoulder tip is pointed and angulated with the upper arm lying away from the chest. The victim classically supports his injured arm with the opposite hand.

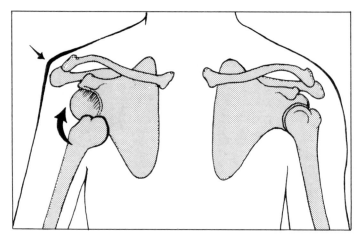

Dislocated shoulder

Before attempting to reduce a dislocated shoulder feel for a radial pulse and test for nerve sensation of touch. Record any abnormal findings because nerves and blood-vessels may get pinched in the armpit (axilla), especially if there is an associated fracture of the neck of the humerus. A pinched circumflex nerve, the commonest injury, causes an area of loss of feeling over the outer upper arm 5 cm below the tip of the shoulder.

Rx: morphine (D.1.4) before attempting reduction.

Act: reassure the victim and help him to relax his shoulder muscles with gentle massage. The shoulder may pop back.

If not – lie the victim face down on an elevated surface for fifteen to thirty minutes with the injured arm hanging down. Tie a weight, like a pack-sack, to the injured wrist in order to give extra traction. This alone may reduce the shoulder.

If it does not – turn the victim over, have an assistant pull the arm gently to an angle of 90° from the body. Then push up gently with both thumbs on the head of the humerus which can be felt in the armpit.

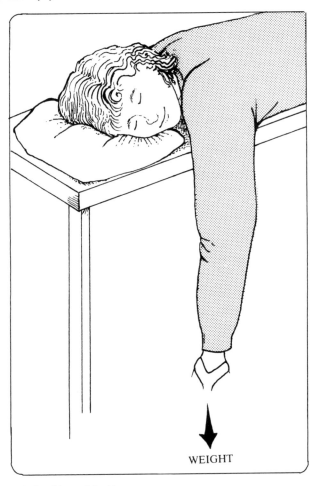

Reducing dislocated shoulder

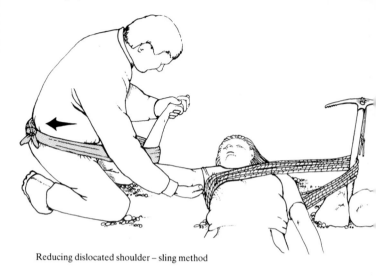

Reducing dislocated shoulder – sling method

If this is unsuccessful try the *two-sling method*. This method is least likely to cause further damage but requires practice. The slings can be made of rolled cloth, a belt, a climbing sling or rope. One sling, well padded, passes under the armpit of the victim's dislocated shoulder and pulls across the body (counter-traction) either towards an assistant kneeling opposite, or to a fixed point like a tree, boulder, or piton in place. Gently move the injured arm 90° away from the trunk (abduction); bend or flex, the elbow to 90°.

Put the other sling first round the crook of the elbow of the injured arm, then round the buttocks of you, the rescuer. Kneel, or squat, beside the victim. With your left hand keep 90° of elbow flexion on the victim's arm, raised to 90° from his trunk. Place your right hand in his armpit feeling for the head of the humerus. Lean back into the loop sling in order to give a strong, steady pull on the victim's arm. Rotate his arm slightly using his forearm to lever the head of the humerus gently over the lip of the shoulder joint rim (glenoid), while pushing lightly with your right hand on the head of the humerus. It should go in with a satisfying pop, and the victim's face will light up with joy.

If he is still suffering try the *Hippocrates method*. Place your own socked foot as high in the victim's armpit as possible. Hold his wrist with both hands and lean backwards with your knee and leg straight. Give a long and steady pull on his arm and push with your heel. This traction will ease his pain immediately. Talk to the victim reassuringly in order to get him to relax.

After at least five minutes traction, gear yourself up mentally for one strong, smooth movement to reduce the shoulder; if you fail the shoulder will go into spasm again and you have lost your chance forever. While maintaining your push-pull on his arm, lever his hand across his body using your heel as a fulcrum. The head of the humerus should slip back into the socket with a slight clunk.

Put the arm in a sling and bind it firmly to the chest. It should be X-rayed as soon as possible, ideally before effecting any of these manoeuvres, in order to exclude a fracture, but this is obviously not possible in the mountains.

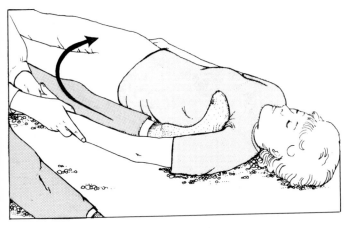

Reducing dislocated shoulder – Hippocrates method

Fracture of the humerus: reduction is unnecessary; use a full arm sling or a collar-and-cuff wrist sling leaving the elbow unsupported to give gravity traction.

Painful shoulder (tendinitis, bursitis, frozen shoulder etc.): many lesions around the shoulder result from bruising, injury, or overuse. Movement is painful and limited.

Rx: naproxen (D.1.2), rest.

ELBOW

Fractures and dislocations around the elbow are common in children. It is difficult to distinguish between the two, so treat as the same. They are especially serious because the brachial artery and nerves crossing the crook of the elbow may be damaged by the broken bone-ends or in attempts at reducing the fracture, a difficult manoeuvre.

Act: if the radial pulse at the wrist is absent always attempt reduction and hope blood-flow will return. If not, splint the arm as you find it and get to hospital fast.

Tennis elbow (lateral epicondlitis): the knob on the outer side of the elbow is tender on lifting a pot, shaking hands or hammering because the origin of the extensor muscles on the back of the forearm is inflamed.

Act: place 1″ tape right round the forearm 2″ below the knob in order to make a false origin for the extensor muscles. Avoid activities that hurt, and be patient for three to six months.

FOREARM

Fracture of the radius and ulna together is usual.

Act: splint with a slab on the back of the forearm including the elbow, and swathe to the body.

WRIST

Colles' fracture, at the further end of radius and ulna: the wrist has the shape of a dinner fork and needs reducing by a surgeon.

Act: splint the forearm with the wrist slightly cocked back. Kramer-wire can be moulded to the shape of the wrist.

'Sprains' often hide an underlying fracture or a ligament tear, which may be serious; so always have them X-rayed.

Scaphoid fracture of the palm: tender over the 'snuffbox' between the tendons of the extended thumb, seen when the thumb is cocked up. It may be complicated when the nearer fragment of bone loses its blood supply and dies (avascular necrosis) as seen on X-ray.

Bennett's fracture (sprained thumb): chip at the base of the thumb metacarpal needs to be screwed into place by a surgeon.

Skier's (gamekeeper's) thumb: disrupted ulnar collateral ligament. The thumb is unstable and the ligament must be repaired surgically.

Tendinitis: the tendons of the wrist hurt and may creak on moving, often as a result of overuse.

   Act: rest, ice, firm bandage

   Rx: naproxen (D.1.2)

HAND

Fractures of the small bones of the hand: splint in a 'boxing glove'. Put a rolled-up sock in the palm of the hand and make a bulky

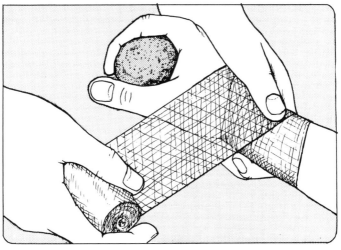

Boxing-glove dressing

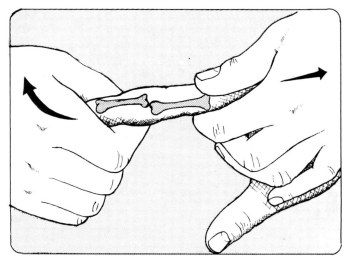

Reducing dislocated finger

dressing with a tensor bandage leaving the fingers open for inspection – a useful dressing for soft tissue injuries of the hand.
Dislocation of the finger or thumb: obvious from its deformity. A straight pull may not be effective because tissue becomes interposed between the ends. Flex the dislocated finger joint then pull while pushing the distal finger (or toe) back in place. Splint the finger to its neighbour.
Tendon and nerve injuries: always serious, flexor tendons in the palm especially so. Surgery is urgent.
Infected hand or fingers: soak in hot water. If pus shows like a boil at the base of the nail (whitlow) or at the apex of the pulp (pulp abscess) first freeze it with ice, then knife it to drain the pus.
    Rx: antibiotic (D.2)
Slivers or splinters: cut a V-wedge over the sliver as far back as possible and try to grasp it with tweezers.
Sliced finger: replace and hold the flap with Steristrips. It may act as a graft and 'take' with full healing.

Avulsion of a finger: keep the part in a plastic bag soaking in saline solution. If a surgeon is reached quickly it may be able to be sewn on again.

LOWER LIMB

HIP OR THIGH
Fracture or dislocation of the head or neck of the femur: the difference may be difficult to tell but is important. In neither condition will the victim be able to walk, and he will have much pain in the hip. A fracture is usually caused by landing on both feet after a fall; the hip is extended and rotated outwards. A dislocation is caused by a force directly on the knee bent at right angles; the hip is flexed and internally rotated and the femur is moved towards the mid-line. It cannot be straightened. Massive contraction of the

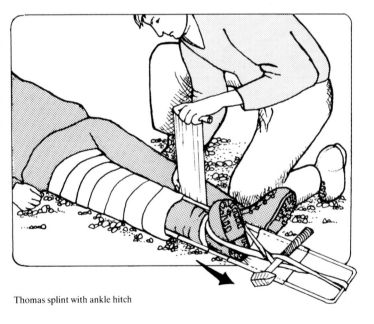

Thomas splint with ankle hitch

buttock and thigh muscles has to be overcome with traction.

Act (fracture): windlass the foot in order to pull the femur straight. A Thomas splint, or one of its modern derivatives, is ideal. Although unlikely to be available, the principle is described here in order to help devise a way of rigging up your own traction device from two pack-frames or other gear at hand.

> Thread the ring of the splint over the injured limb until it abuts against the pubic bone high up in the crotch. An assistant pulls on the victim's foot. The leg rests on supporting slings secured with safety-pins between the arms of the splint. Tie an ankle-hitch over his boot with a bandage and secure it to the cross end-piece of the splint. Increase traction on the leg by windlassing the bandage, but beware not to overtighten it. If the victim complains of pain around the ankle-hitch, slacken the tension. With his boot on you cannot see the colour of his toes nor feel their temperature, so beware of impeding the circulation.
>
> If you cannot make a traction device, tie two ice-axes together to make a splint from armpit to ankle. Pad the picks well. Place binders round the whole body and bandage the bad leg to the good one, with lots of padding between them.

Act (dislocation): reduction may be impossible without anaesthetic and muscle relaxation but is worth a try. A Thomas

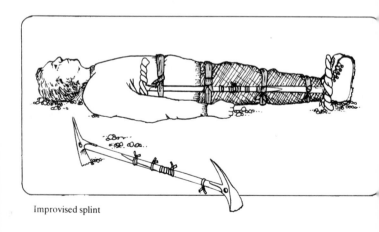

Improvised splint

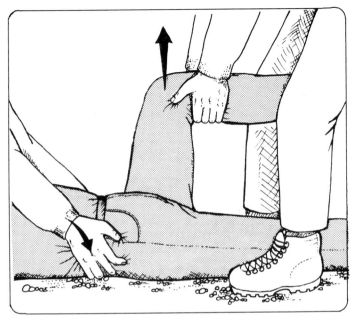

Reducing dislocated hip

splint is useless for reducing a hip, and would be impossible to position due to the swelling. With an assistant pressing down on the wings of the victim's pelvis, bend his knee to 90° and steady his foot between your knees. Give a long, strong pull upwards and gently rotate the hip. The ball of the femur should slip into the socket of the pelvis.

Trochanteric bursitis: pain develops over the protuberance of the hip, increases on walking.

   Act: rest

   Rx: naproxen (D.1.2)

Ruptured saphenous vein: causes dramatic bruising and swelling on the inside of the thigh. It will subside unaided.

KNEE

Knee fracture and dislocation: are rare and only result from violent force.

Patella fracture: the knee is swollen and tender over the knee-cap where a dent may be felt. Patella dislocation is usually recurrent and the victim knows how to replace it.

Ligament or meniscus tears: are difficult to differentiate. The knee is swollen and feels unstable. Pain is felt particularly when pressing over the joint line on the injured side.

Act: hold the knee straight and immobile by firm support with a crêpe bandage from thigh to ankle. The bulkier the dressing the steadier it will be held.

Bursitis: pain and tenderness are felt in front of the patella (housemaids); below the patella (clergymen); or behind the hollow (climbers).

Act: rest

Rx: naproxen (D.1.2)

LOWER LEG

Fractured tibia or fibula: usually both bones break, and the leg is deformed and painful. Walking is impossible.

Act: splint from above the knee to below the ankle and evacuate to a surgeon.

Ruptured gastrocnemius or Achilles tendon: the victim feels as though he has been booted in the mid-calf or above the heel. Walking is difficult and he cannot tip-toe.

Act: the calf will heal on its own; the Achilles may need surgery.

Shin splints: embodies a multitude of aches felt in the lower leg after over-use by hypochondriacal athletes. Rest is of the essence.

Thrombo-phlebitis: the calf is tender and flexing the foot towards the knee causes pain in the calf. The danger is of a clot shooting to the lungs (embolus).

Act: rest.

Rx: analgesics (D.1) and antibiotics (D.2), until symptoms subside.

ANKLE

Sprains and fractures of the ankle occur by tripping over boulders or
falling from a height. They are difficult to distinguish, especially a
lateral malleolus fracture which is common in skiing and may be
diagnosed as a twisted ankle. Both are swollen and painful. A
fracture makes walking most unpleasant. If the heels hurt, suspect a
fractured calcaneum and examine the spine as it may also have been
injured in the fall. A fracture-chip off the lateral malleolus (the
outer part of the bony ankle) is common in skiing and may be
mistaken for a sprain or a twisted ankle.

Act: pillow-splint a fracture with a down jacket; splint a sprain
firmly with tape making a figure-of-eight around the ankle.

FOOT

Fractures of the small bones occur when a boulder drops on the foot,
or after long marching – usually the second metatarsal. They are
painful but not serious and can be strapped. The victim should walk
off the mountain if possible; dallying may mean being benighted
with the peril that goes with an unplanned bivouac. To evacuate
someone by stretcher is slow, laborious and often dangerous. A
broken arm should not hinder descent, but a fractured leg will
probably be too painful to walk on and the victim will have to be
carried. Keep reviewing the condition of the person and his limb as
you descend. He may need a dressing loosened, a splint adjusted, a
pee, or another dose of pain-killer.

Ingrowing toe-nail: always cut toe-nails straight across to prevent a
sliver at the side digging in and becoming painfully infected.

Act: warm salt soaks, cut a V-wedge in the middle of the nail.

Rx: antibiotic (D.2).

PELVIS

Fractured pelvis: falling from a height is the commonest cause of a
climber crushing the ring of pelvic bones. The pelvis is surrounded
by many muscles and hollow spaces so a severe fracture may not be
obvious; the person's only complaint may be of pain round the hips
and difficulty in walking. Several pints of blood can seep away into
the tissues unnoticed before he suddenly collapses from shock. He

may rupture his urethra or bladder as a result of the fractured pelvis.

Act: pad the crotch with soft wool clothing and put a firm supporting binder round the upper thighs; bandage the knees and feet together to prevent the legs moving on the pelvis. Give analgesics and carry him off the mountain gently on a stretcher.

Abdomen

All tender bellies need a surgeon; telling one condition from another needs skill, but your careful, written observations will help him. Until help can be reached use intravenous fluids, antibiotics – and hope.

EXAMINING THE ABDOMEN
Ask: where is the pain? (the areas where pain and tenderness are usually felt overlie the organs; to describe the pain divide the abdomen into quarters – right and left, upper and lower, flanks to the side, loins behind). When and how did it start? (exact time, sudden or gradual). Nature of pain (dull, aching, sharp, crampy) and any change? Has pain moved? Does it radiate to another area (to the back, shoulders, genitals)? Appetite loss, indigestion, nausea, vomiting? Diarrhoea, constipation? Peeing more frequent or burning? Blood in the urine or stool?

Look: first at his face. Is he well or ill, pale or flushed, hot or cold, frowning in pain or calm and relaxed? Remove clothing so you can see from chest to thigh. Scars of previous surgery? Tongue moist or dry (as in dehydration or mouth-breathing), clean or furred with smelly breath (as in appendicitis)? Does the abdomen rise with normal breathing, is it held rigid with the lower chest doing all the work, is it swollen or distended? Local swelling, especially in the hernial areas?

Feel: the pulse, and temperature of the forehead using the back of the fingers. Feel gently in all quarters of the belly with the flat of a warm hand; don't dig with your fingers or he'll tense and you will learn nothing. Does the abdomen let your hand sink in or does it feel rigid, 'guarding' the contents? Press in one spot; does it hurt in another? Watch his face all the while for a grimace that suggests tenderness. Only a large or solid mass will be identifiable by feel; detecting a small mass requires much experience. Gently feel the hernia areas in the groin, the scrotum and the testicles.

Listen: for normal gurgling bowel sounds with an ear placed

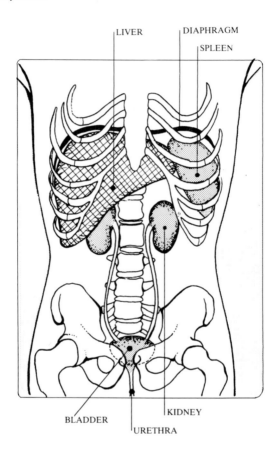

Abdominal organs

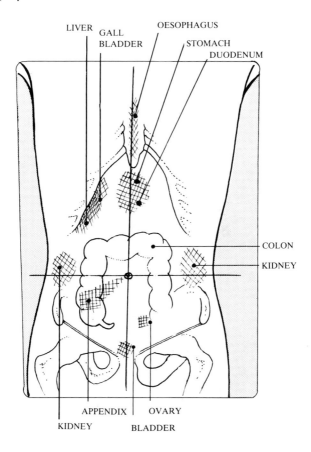

Areas (approximate) where abdominal organ pain is felt

against his belly for at least three minutes: tinkling sounds tell that the bowel is moving; silence suggests paralysis (ileus) possibly due to obstruction or peritonitis.

Draw a picture to record all findings.

Acute belly-ache can occur in the fit, young, and healthy. The most serious cause is appendicitis, which if neglected, can be deadly.

ACUTE APPENDICITIS

Appendicitis is easy to diagnose once all the classical signs are manifest; yet in its early stages it can be similar to several other conditions that cause abdominal pain. The finger-like appendix lies in the right lower-quarter of the abdomen. Its variable position in relation to the large bowel, and its stage of inflammation, account for the variety of signs it presents.

Symptoms and signs
Pain commonly starts round the umbilicus and after about six hours shifts to the right lower-quarter. The idea of food is revolting, the victim feels queasy and refuses fried egg and chips. Vomiting usually occurs after the onset of central pain and before it moves to the right side. Walking hurts in the right groin and he prefers to lie still with his legs drawn up.

Look: he is unwell and flushed with fever; if the appendix perforates the pain eases and he looks pale and shocked owing to peritonitis. The pulse races. The tongue is furred and the breath stinks. A scar may suggest that the appendix has already been snatched, so ask about previous surgery. If it has gone heave a sigh of relief because the diagnosis will be easier.

Feel: muscles in the right lower-quarter guard the tender contents of his belly, whereas the left side remains soft and empty. Pressing more deeply where it hurts, and, once only, releasing the pressure suddenly, may evoke an 'ouch!' (rebound tenderness). Bowel sounds are absent if peritonitis has spread.

Act: an inflamed appendix can burst within twenty-four to thirty-six hours, spilling pus into the belly and causing peritonitis, which may kill. If a surgeon cannot be reached swiftly, stop feeding the person by mouth because drinking will make him vomit, and give intravenous fluids.

> 'Drip-and-suck' should tide the victim over till surgery. Use an intravenous infusion with normal saline or Ringer's solution run at about 3 litres over twenty-four hours, and a naso-gastric tube passed through the nose (or mouth if not possible) into the stomach and taped in place. Suck out the contents hourly.

Rx: double doses of broad-spectrum antibiotic, cephalosporin (D.2.1) i/v would be best, but i/m or oral route would do. This time-honoured ship-board treatment works. Be generous with pain-killers.

If the victim is not cured by this regime he may develop a mass with the appendix walled off by omentum (the fat-laden membrane that hangs from the bowel). This forms an abscess, like a time-bomb wrapped in a protective coat for later dismantling by a surgeon. The worst scenario is when the appendix bursts spilling pus into the peritoneum (peritonitis); then metronidazole (D.2.3) should be added to the antibiotic regime.

The following conditions mimic appendicitis and have to be excluded when faced with acute low belly-ache, but in every case a surgeon should be consulted as soon as possible, because an accurate diagnosis is very difficult to make on a mountainside. They are arranged roughly in order of commonness.

CONSTIPATION
Caused by inadequate drinking, lack of fresh fruit, eating dehydrated food, and medication containing morphine or codeine. Prove with a laxative suppository or an enema; like clearing a log jam, it's best approached from below. An impacted, rock-hard stool may be the result of dehydration and constipation owing to being storm-bound in a tent and not melting enough snow in order to drink. If the stool has to be removed push a greased finger as high in the rectum as possible breaking the hard stool and withdrawing it in pieces. A soapy water enema helps to flush out the residue.

GASTRO-ENTERITIS

Crampy pain, profuse and watery diarrhoea, nausea and vomiting are usual. The story may be of eating strange food (oysters, or Tibetan tea) or of other members of the party being similarly stricken. Giardiasis is a cause where beavers live in the water and also in the Himalaya and other wild regions.

Act: avoid eating, drink plenty. Diarrhoea will probably cease in twenty-four to forty-eight hours. If not

Rx: loperamide (D.9.3); metronidazole (D.2.3) for giardia.

URINARY TRACT INFECTION

The victim, commonly female, pees frequently (every fifteen to thirty minutes), and it feels like passing powdered glass. The urine is murky and smelly and may be tinged with blood. Pain and tenderness are felt in the loin (kidney infection, pyelitis), or above the pubis (bladder infection, cystitis), which mimics an inflamed appendix in contact with the ureter or bladder. Despite a high fever she shakes with chills.

Rx: fluids in plenty with baking soda added in order to make the urine alkaline and less clement to acid-loving E. coli; a broad-spectrum antibiotic, co-trimoxazole (D.2.2).

STONE IN THE KIDNEY OR URETER

So long as a stone remains in the kidney only a dull ache is felt in the loin. Agonizing colic ('the worst pain I've ever felt') occurs when a small stone passes down the ureter which connects kidneys and bladder. Small stones, like small dogs, make most noise. The victim rolls around with steady pain, which starts in the loin and moves towards the groin and often into the genitals. Pain comes in waves, builds to a crescendo with vomiting, and then dies down leaving a dull ache. Urine is passed frequently and may be blood-stained.

Act: drink lots in order to flush out the stone, take strong pain-killers, and meditate whilst waiting for the passing of the stone.

ACUTE GALL-BLADDER

Constant severe pain, felt high under the right ribs, travels through to the back, to the bottom of the lower right shoulder blade, or to the right shoulder tip. Fatty foods cause indigestion. A low-slung gall-bladder may give pain down to the right lower-quarter, like appendicitis. However, it is more likely to be confused with a peptic ulcer or an inflamed oesophagus. Yellow jaundice suggests a stone is obstructing the flow of bile, causing pale stools and dark urine.

Act: most attacks subside without surgery, so rest and give limited fluids.

Rx: codeine (D.1.3), (not morphine which constricts the bile-duct exit), and antibiotics (D.2).

WOMEN'S PROBLEMS
Pain from the right ovary or right fallopian tube can mimic appendicitis.

Ovary pain – ask any woman complaining of low belly-ache the date of her last period, and whether she could be pregnant. The pain may be just her normal pre-menstrual 'curse' pains which are sometimes quite disabling. If the date is exactly half-way between her periods she may be ovulating normally. Acute pain and tenderness lingering for a few hours may be due to slight bleeding from the ovarian follicle into the peritoneum (mittelschmertz).

Salpingitis – infection of the fallopian tubes is usually accompanied by smelly vaginal discharge. Fever is high and pain is felt usually on both sides low down, but it may be over the appendix only.

If she is pregnant beware of:

Abortion (miscarriage) – the story is of a missed period, heavy vaginal bleeding, and generalized cramps with passing of clots.

Rx: [ergometrine] 0.25 mg. i/m.

Ectopic pregnancy – a rare condition when a pregnancy develops outside the womb in one or other fallopian tube, which can suddenly burst causing profuse bleeding into the belly.

Act: only surgery avails; i/v fluids may help meanwhile.

INTESTINAL OBSTRUCTION

Any part of the bowel, large or small, may become obstructed by a multitude of causes, mostly too academic to discuss here. But look for a scar from previous surgery suggesting adhesions or a hernia that may have twisted.

The bowel may distend, strangulate, become gangrenous and burst leading to fatal peritonitis. Any obstruction on the right side of the belly may simulate appendicitis. The features are of a sick-looking person with pain, vomiting, distension, and absolute constipation.

Rx: drip-and-suck, pain-killers (D.1), and antibiotics; cephalosporin (D.2.1) and metronidazole (D.2.3).

PEPTIC ULCER

Ulcers in the stomach or duodenum can exist for years without causing more than vague indigestion and discomfort in the pit of the stomach coming on one to two hours after eating. Avoid fried foods, coffee, alcohol and cigarettes, but drink milk. An ulcer may bleed or perforate suddenly and catastrophically.

Rx: aluminium hydroxide (D.9.1), famotidine (D.9.2).

Bleeding – the victim feels faint and sweaty, vomits bright-red or coffee-ground blood (haematemesis) and becomes shocked. Diarrhoea may follow some hours later with dark, tarry stools (melaena).

Act: drip-and-suck until it is possible to replace blood with blood; Rx: famotidine (D.9.2).

Perforation – sudden pain in the upper abdomen, can mimic a heart attack or a perforated appendix. 3–4 litres of noxious, toxic stomach contents are spilled spreading bacteria throughout the belly and causing peritonitis. The pain steadily worsens with vomiting and a rising pulse. He may begin to improve deceptively before collapsing with a tender rigid abdomen. Breathing is shallow and he looks, and is, deathly.

Act: drip-and-suck; evacuate immediately.

Rx: morphine (D.1.4), cephalosporin (D.2.1), metronidazole (D.2.3).

Hernia

Gut or omentum may protrude through the muscular abdominal wall, usually in the groin following the strain of carrying heavy loads. It may slide back on lying down, with the help of firm manual pressure. But gut may be nipped off and become strangulated, gangrenous and perforate. A tense, tender swelling in the groin cannot be pushed back; the victim vomits copiously, has griping pains, a distended belly and is shocked.

In a tent north of Dhaulagiri in the Himalayas I once came across a Tibetan lama who looked just like this. After a dose of morphine and a mug of 'rakshi' spirits I tried to squeeze the hernia back – to no avail. With two Sherpas holding him down, some local anaesthetic, another monk chanting mantras and a small suture kit I operated on him, untwisted the bowel and sewed him up. Ten minutes later a thunderous fart announced our luck and his life. Such surgery is neither recommended nor approved by the Royal Colleges.

Testicle

Sudden pain without a story of injury is likely to be due either to acute inflammation, or to torsion of the testicle, which must be untwisted urgently.

Act: support the scrotum in a tight pair of underpants well padded with cotton-wool. Make a cautious gentle attempt at unwinding the torsion and don't make him laugh.

Rx: cephalosporin (D.2.1).

Piles (haemorrhoids)

Mountaineers are prone to piles (like varicose veins of the anus), especially at high altitudes. Straining at stool, or carrying heavy loads with consequent overbreathing, raises the pressure within the abdomen causing piles to pop out. Always uncomfortable and inconvenient when prolapsed, they feel like grapes at the anal margin and can be very painful. Bright blood on the toilet paper after passing stool heralds piles, and slimy discharge causes maddening itch.

Act: have troublesome piles shrunk by a surgeon's needle (surprisingly painless) before setting out on a trip. If already embarked, take bran to soften the stool and drink enough fluid to prevent constipation. Avoid morphine or codeine. Keep scrupulously clean because soiling with faeces causes maddening itch.

Rx: bismuth subgallate (D.9.5) haemorrhoidal cream or suppository.

Push prolapsed piles back inside the anus quickly to avoid them swelling and staying out. Dropping your trousers at 7,000 m (20,000 ft) in a blizzard is bad enough, but having prolapsed piles as well is the ultimate misery.

11   Abdominal injury

The abdomen houses 9 m (28 ft) of gut and several major organs;
liver, spleen, kidneys, bladder (see page 118). The entire cavity and
the organs themselves are enveloped in a thin membrane of
peritoneum, which allows gut to move around without friction.
Peritoneum senses pain when stretched or irritated by noxious fluids
or blood.

Serious injury to the abdomen, whether blunt (closed) or sharp
(penetrating), may cause internal bleeding or leakage of gut
contents, faeces, pus or urine; any or all of which cause peritonitis.
So be alert, even after a minor blow, for possible internal mischief
not immediately manifest. Surgery is the treatment for most
abdominal injuries.

Closed abdominal injury

Ask: about the nature of the object causing the injury, and the way
the accident happened, for example, falling across a rock, or onto
an ice-axe.

SYMPTOMS AND SIGNS
Pain – varies greatly; if severe the victim lies quite still. Pain is
usually felt first around the umbilicus but spreads and settles in the
region of the injured organ. Noxious fluids in contact with the under
surface of the diaphragm irritate the phrenic nerve referring pain to
one or both shoulder tips.

Tenderness – is general with guarding over the injured organs. If
peritonitis spreads, the abdominal muscles feel rigid, like pressing
on a board. Further pressure causes pain, especially when the
examining hand is suddenly removed (rebound tenderness).

Shock – is always present after internal bleeding. The victim is pale,
sweaty, and cold with a rapid, feeble pulse. If there is no external
bleeding, look to the abdomen for the cause. Shock is uncommon in
head injury.

Vomiting – preceded by nausea is a constant sign of abdominal mischief, especially peritonitis. Bleeding from the stomach is rare in abdominal trauma so if bright-red, fresh blood appears in the vomit, look for an injured nose, mouth or tongue.

Blood in the urine – damage to the kidneys or bladder is likely; blood at the end of the penis suggests injury to the urethra.

Breathing – is quiet, using the lower chest with the abdomen held still.

Act: reassure: if the victim is flippant about an injury you suspect is not trivial, warn him of possible serious consequences and descend as soon as possible.

Rest: completely; allow only sips of water by mouth as he may vomit, but a dry person is a restless one. Don't worry about fluid in his stomach; this is the hospital anaesthetist's problem, not yours, and he can deal with it.

Record: all observations every half-hour on paper, especially the pulse rate and any change in his condition.

Rx: morphine (D.1.4) relieves pain and allays anxiety, but it causes vomiting; so also promethazine (D.3.1). Do not withhold analgesics for fear of masking pain from the doctor who will try to diagnose him later; he can always reverse the effects of morphine with an antagonist, for example naloxone. Always write the drug name, the dose and the time given on a label and attach it to the victim for the information of the receiving doctor.

NB: Infection: the stage is set because blood is an ideal medium for growing bugs, and spilt intestinal contents are teeming with bacteria. Give large doses of broad spectrum antibiotics (D.2).

SPECIFIC CLOSED INJURIES

Spleen – quite trivial force, like falling across an ice-axe, can rupture the spleen. When the lower left ribs are fractured the underlying spleen may be impaled. So always suspect abdominal organ rupture after a chest injury, especially on the left. Progressively severe bleeding with shock is usual after rupture, but silent symptomless bleeding may continue from several hours to three weeks beneath the enfolding caspsule which stretches and suddenly bursts, spilling blood into the peritoneum. The victim becomes deeply shocked. Therefore anyone suffering an abdominal injury on a mountain, however mild, should descend because of the danger of secondary haemorrhage.

Liver – caused by a crushing blow to the upper abdomen or fracture of the lower right ribs. Minor tears often stop bleeding; in massive injury it continues unabated. Occasionally a subcapsular haematoma develops (similar to the spleen) with sudden catastrophic bleeding after a delay of some hours.

Kidney – caused by a direct blow in the loin or flank, possibly with a fracture of the twelfth rib. Pain is local when bleeding is contained within the capsule of the kidney, and blood is usually seen in the urine (haematuria). Many cases resolve with rest alone.

Urethra – a tear occurs either when a fractured segment of pelvis to which the urethra is tethered is pulled apart, or after falling astride a solid object like a fence or onto a rock.

The victim, most commonly a man, has severe pain in the crotch, which is badly bruised between the scrotum and the anus. Look for fresh blood at the end of the penis. He will be unable to pass urine. The bladder becomes distended some hours later, can be felt above the pubic bone and is very uncomfortable. Instead of passing down the damaged urethra, urine and blood may spread up into the muscle planes of the lower abdomen or the perineum which readily become infected.

Act: Rx: broad spectrum antibiotic (D.2) immediately. Do nothing else for twenty-four hours. No harm can come from inactivity, but a lot of damage may ensue from attempting to pass a catheter, because the few remaining strands by which the urethra can re-canalize itself may be broken. Leave the catheter to a waterworks specialist because by meddling now it may be irreparable later.

If far from help and if his bladder swells after waiting twenty-four hours, plunge a wide-bore sterile needle through the cleansed skin of the abdominal wall in the mid-line 2 cm (1″) above the pubic bone at least 5 cm (2″) deep (bladder is close against abdominal wall nothing else intervening at this point) and let urine spurt out. Repeated stabs, perhaps every eight hours, or whenever the bladder appears full, are less likely to cause infection than leaving an indwelling needle or canula.

Bladder – rupture is rare.

Act: Rx: antibiotics (D.2) and supra-pubic drainage (as above) will tide him over until he can reach a surgeon.

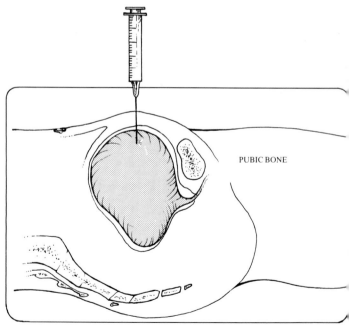

PUBIC BONE

Supra-pubic bladder drain

Open abdominal injury

In the rare event of an open wound from a knife, ice-axe or
gun-shot, guts or fatty omentum may protrude, a horrendous sight.
Do not try to push them back inside, but cover the wound with a
clean, preferably sterile, damp dressing. If the instrument that
caused the injury is still in the wound, and if you can reach help
quickly, leave it there as, like the Dutch boy's finger in the dyke, it
may be plugging the hole. However, if it is in a major blood-vessel
it may wriggle free during transport, and this would be fatal, so you
may have to take a chance and remove it.

A small puncture wound of the skin should cause as much anxiety
as an obvious gash. You can only guess whether the instrument has
nicked the skin and penetrated muscle, or whether it has pierced an
internal organ. A long sharp object, like a knife, which punctures
the skin can be withdrawn leaving barely a mark, but a punctured
bowel may seal over temporarily and leak noxious fluid later,
becoming fatal. Most surgeons assume that a puncture wound has
penetrated the abdominal cavity, until proved otherwise, and
operate forthwith.

12   Burns and heat injury

Minor burns

These involve less than fifteen per cent of the body surface area and are a painful nuisance.

SUNBURN

Sunburn is the commonest burn seen in climbers. The sun is a stealthy enemy; it reflects strongly off water, sand and snow. Ultraviolet rays penetrate hazy cloud, and the higher the altitude the more they burn; each 300 m altitude rise adds four per cent to the rays' intensity. Those with fair skin, red hair or freckles are more liable to sunburn. Tanning is the best skin protection but people tan at varying speed. Rationing sunlight on the skin is the cheapest, most effective way to avoid sunburn and to tan. Wear a wide-brimmed hat or a peaked cap with a neck cover. Sun-glasses should have blinker side-pieces and nose shields. Lips and noses burn, especially on the underside, from ultraviolet light reflected off snow. Unlike sunbathing on the beach, it is more difficult to cut down the length of sun exposure on a mountain. Falling asleep in the sun is a sure way to fry, and even a sola topi worn at midday will not save mad dogs or Englishmen.

Sun-creams and lotions act as a screen to the burning parts of the ultraviolet spectrum; none speed *le bronzage*, and with excessive sun they just act as fat for frying. Para-aminobenzoic acid is the base of most sun-screens. The Sun Protection Factor (SPF) should be marked on the bottle from 1 to 20; the higher the number, the greater the protection.

Act: find shade if skin goes shrimp-pink and feels prickly and hot. Baking soda compresses or calamine soothe.

Rx: anti-histamines (D.3) allay itching; avoid topical local anaesthetic and anti-histamine creams which can cause sensitivity reactions. Badly burnt skin goes bright lobster-red and blisters.

betamethasone steroid cream (D.11.1) helps.

paracetamol (D.1.1) for fever. Severe general body upset

(hyperthermia see page 143) with headache, vomiting and fainting may ensue. Cool with ice and fanning.

FLAME BURN

Open air – flame-burns and scalds go hand-in-hand with hot cooking pans, boiling water and hot fat. The flash of flame from petrol or gas ignited in open air passes in a second; the skin turns brown or black, but the burn will probably be superficial and heal within a couple of weeks. Flaming clothing continues to burn the skin for several seconds, often causing a deep burn which takes weeks, or months, to heal and may need skin-grafting. Some synthetic fabrics like nylon and polypropylene melt and burn deeply. Fireproof synthetic materials are labelled as such. Wool and natural fibre do not hold flame, so the burn is delayed reaching the skin. However, wool keeps boiling water in contact with the skin thus prolonging the scalding time. Boiling water, and a frying-pan fat aflame on bare skin, often burn deeply.

Enclosed space – explosions within a tent, snow cave or camper van produce hot gases which are inhaled, burning the air passages and lungs, often fatally. Liquid propane gas is heavier than air and, when spilled, settles on the floor. If ignited by a match, a spark or another stove it explodes.

FRICTION BURNS

Deep friction burns to the hands, neck and back can occur when a climber tries to hold a falling companion, or when roping down.

ELECTRICAL BURNS

Deeper and more extensive than at first sight, electrical burns heal slowly, especially at the point where the current enters and leaves the body.

Lightning – is a danger on summits and ridges, and when sitting under a tree or other conductor. It usually strikes the head causing unconsciousness and deafness for one to two weeks. If the heart is struck the victim may die of ventricular fibrillation. With a direct strike the burn spreads over the skin surface making a fern-like pattern; an indirect burn is caused by superheated air near the object struck.

Car battery – burns may occur when booster cables are connected wrongly.

CHEMICAL BURNS
Chemical burns are usually caused by lime or acid. Car batteries may explode violently if a spark ignites escaping hydrogen gas. Immediately wash burned skin, especially the eyes, with copious water.

ACTION FOR MINOR BURNS
Apart from the specific treatments mentioned, minor burns are generally best left open to the air to dry, or covered with a small sterile dressing, if such is appropriate. They usually heal quickly and completely.

Major burns

Major burns cause two main problems, tissue damage and fluid loss; together these lead to 'burn shock' similar to the shock that follows severe bleeding. Emotional shock (fear, pain, and fainting) that follows the burning accident compounds and worsens clinical shock. Major burns always need fluid replacement.

Tissue damage
A burn is a wound; the depth of tissue destroyed is important in determining the time a wound will take to heal, and whether skin-grafting will be necessary.

AREA OF BURN
Severity of the burn is assessed by measuring the burned body-surface area (bsa) irrespective of depth, according to the 'rule of 9s'. The palm area of the victim's hand, not the rescuer's, is one per cent bsa.

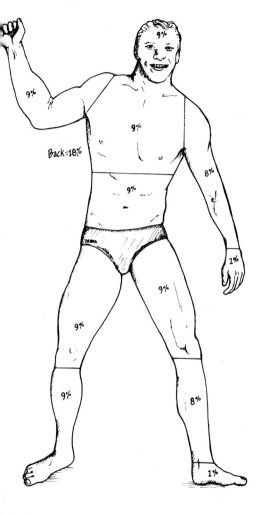

– minor burns (less than fifteen per cent bsa) heal unaided.
– major burns (more than fifteen per cent bsa in adults) are a threa
to life with consequences stretching far beyond the burn wound
itself. In children a major burn is more than ten per cent bsa,
because children have a greater body surface area in relation to
their weight.

DEPTH OF BURN
Partial-thickness (superficial) – a partial-thickness burn penetrates
the germinal epithelium, where new cells that spread out to form
new epidermis skin are generated, harming it to a variable extent.
Partial-thickness burns usually heal unaided in seven to twenty-one

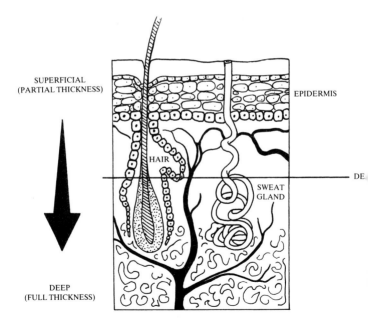

Burn skin depth

days if kept clean and dry. Infection delays healing and may convert a partial-thickness burn into one of full-thickness.

Full-thickness (deep) – most full-thickness burns extend through the germinal layer of cells destroying nerves and blood-vessels, hair follicles and sweat glands that lie in that layer. The skin will not re-generate on its own and will usually need skin-grafting. The colour of burned skin is a poor guide to burn depth, better tests are:
– pinprick; if the victim can feel the prick of a sterile needle firm enough to draw blood (light touch is not enough), the burn is superficial. In a full-thickness burn nerves are destroyed so pain is absent.
– pressure; if the skin feels leathery and firm on pressure, it is deeply burned – a useful test in scalds where the skin looks pink. If the colour returns quickly when pressure is removed, the burn is superficial.

Exuded plasma and coagulated tissue form a slough, which hardens to a dry crust (eschar) if left open to the air and kept clean of infection. Healing goes on under the crust which eventually separates leaving a raw area (granulation tissue). Early skin-grafting in hospital can prevent the hideous disabling deformities that are a common sequel to major burns.

Act: *Cool* – immediately douse any burn, whatever the cause, with cold water or snow for at least ten minutes. Cooling halts burning and eases pain. Before focusing attention on the victim's burn wound, attend to the airway and treat pain.

Airway – to lose a burn victim from airway block is tragic, because it is usually avoidable (see page 47).

> An endotracheal tube should be passed early rather than late. A tracheotomy may be needed on reaching hospital, but never in the field.

Pain – not only is pain unpleasant, but also it aggravates shock. Reassure the victim and give enough drugs to kill his pain. A superficial burn will usually hurt as the nerve-endings in the epidermis will be intact; they are destroyed in a deep burn which may be free of pain.

Rx: morphine (D.1.4).

Managing a major burn in the wilds will be very difficult. The ideal treatment is explained here, knowing you will not be able to carry it out fully. Do not despair just because you are in a remote mountain range several days, or weeks away from help. Ingenuity and common sense must prevail.

THE BURN WOUND
Whatever the cause of the burn, the immediate care of the burn wound, whether major or minor, is the same – refinements in treatment come later.

Cool – douse in cold water or snow.

Undress – remove clothing in order to examine the full extent of the burn. If charred fabric sticks to the skin leave it in place because pulling it away may restart bleeding; it will be sterile anyway because of the heat. Remove rings and jewellery which may constrict the circulation after swelling.

Clean – wash with plenty of soap and water. With sterile forceps remove dead tissue that comes away easily. Irrigate chemical burns (especially lime in the eyes) with plain water for at least ten minutes.

Record – draw a careful diagram of the area of the burn (rule of 9s) and the depth of burning (pinprick test) in order to follow the progress of healing during the long days ahead. Ask how the accident occurred, and what steps were taken to extinguish the cause of the burn.

Dressing – cover the wound with clean, sterile, dry linen or non-stick dressing. A dressing acts as a mechanical barrier to infection and absorbs exudate from the wound, allowing it to dry

and start healing. Apply a pad of absorbent cotton wool on top of
the dressing in order to soak up exuded fluid. Two layers of plain
paraffin gauze may be used next to the burn. The dressing should
extend at least a handsbreadth beyond the edge of the burn. Finally,
wrap a crêpe bandage evenly over the dressing; firmly enough to
keep it in place, but not so tight as to restrict circulation. Do not
smear the burn with butter, burn-creams, or patent potions which
confuse the picture and make dressings stick fast. Avoid antibiotic
creams because they encourage the growth of resistant bacteria.

If there is no immediate chance of reaching help, a burn dressing
can be left in place for up to a week provided it remains dry and free
of infection. Repeated peeking at the wound lays open a path for
infection to enter. As soon as plasma soaks through the dressing,
replace the outer absorbent packing only, leaving the immediate
dressing in place. If it smells foul, has a pussy discharge, if pain and
redness develop in skin away from the burn, or if the victim's
temperature rises undo the dressing completely and start again,
because these are signs of infection. Ideally, when exposed to open
air, a burn wound will dry forming a crusting scab, (escar or
carapace) under which healing proceeds free from bacteria. But
open exposure will be impossible out on a mountain so the wound
needs to be dressed.

Blisters – leave small blisters alone and use a moleskin doughnut to
keep off pressure while they heal. Leave large blisters intact if
possible because they form a skin roof and a good sterile enclosure.
If the blister is in a place that will rub, it will break anyway so
puncture the blebs with a sterile needle or blade. Careful lancing on
the first day can be quite painless. Keep the resulting open wound
scrupulously clean as infection can easily creep in. If blisters break
by themselves and become infected they are very painful.

Rx: a broad-spectrum antibiotic (D.2) for at least ten days if
infection supervenes.

analgesics; dressing changes are agony, so give a strong
pain-killer before starting – codeine (D.1.3) or morphine (D.1.4).

tetanus toxoid; get a booster dose as soon as help is reached.

All treatment is aimed towards keeping the burn wound clean and avoiding infection. In hospital skin-grafting may be needed to treat areas of full-thickness burning. If the wound is clean this can be done soon after arrival.

Fluid loss

Damaged capillaries leak plasma, the fluid portion of blood, which exudes from the raw surface, forms blisters under the outer layers of the skin, and collects round the burn in swollen tissues. The body compensates for loss of plasma from a burn by withdrawing fluid from regions where it is not needed instantly, vessels in the periphery of the skin and in the gut clamp down so blood pools in the central circulation, and compulsive thirst and drinking makes up for some of the lost fluid – all the early signs of shock.

After a major burn plasma must be replaced quickly, if possible intravenously, in order to avoid shock; the longer the delay the worse the outcome. Severe bleeding causes immediate shock in proportion to the blood lost; but burn-shock develops slowly over several hours owing to accumulated toxic products of tissue destruction and plasma loss. The victim appears deceptively well soon after the accident and then deteriorates over the next twenty-four to thirty-six hours. Some red cells are destroyed in the scorched skin, others pass into the circulation and fragment later leading to anaemia. The breakdown products of blood cells lodge in the kidney and give the urine a red-brown colour.

Act: measure the burned area accurately according to the rule of 9s, paying attention only to the area, not the depth of burning. Replace fluid according to your estimate of his needs by judging the victim's condition.

After a major burn an intravenous drip is the best way of restoring fluid balance. If you are out in the wilds other routes must be considered. They cannot overload the circulation, as can intravenous fluid, but are less efficient.

ORAL
The victim should drink 3 litres daily if possible, taking small sips rather than big gulps in order to avoid vomiting. Water will do, but

the WHO formula (D.18) may replace enough electrolyte, glucose and water to keep the victim of a fifty per cent burn alive.

RECTAL

A greased wide-bore tube is inserted as high up the rectum as possible, preferably about 15 cm (7″) from the anus. Fluid of any sort is run in as fast as the victim can retain it without overflow.

NASO-GASTRIC

If the victim cannot drink, a greased 14 mm diameter naso-gastric tube is passed into the stomach via the nose (difficult sometimes to turn the bend at the back of the pharynx), or through the mouth (may make him gag and vomit). To tell when the tube is lying in the stomach, watch for fluid in an attached funnel start to flow, and gurgling can be heard with a stethoscope or an ear placed over the upper abdomen.

SUBCUTANEOUS

The needle of an intravenous apparatus is inserted under the loose skin on the front of the chest or abdomen. The needle lies in the plane between skin and muscle where fluid spreads and is slowly absorbed. 3 litres should be put in each twenty-four hours.

INTRAVENOUS FLUID

Choose a large vein as the drip may have to last several days. The best replacement fluid is human plasma reconstituted with sterile water as it contains all the essential proteins; Ringer's lactate or normal saline will do temporarily.

The amount of fluid needed is 4–5 ml/kg body weight/percentage body surface area burned/twenty-four hours at the rate of ½ the volume in the first eight-hour period, ¼ in each of the next eight-hour periods. This relates to the time of the burn and therefore initial fluid replacement must catch up and may have to be given rapidly. Thereafter give enough fluid to produce 30–50 ml of urine each hour.

Special burn sites

FACE, EYELIDS, EYES

Most facial burns can be left exposed to the air. But the lax tissues of the lids swell and may close the victim's eyes; he needs reassurance that he is not going blind. Burns of the cornea, the window of the eye, are uncommon because blinking usually occurs before the flame reaches the eye. Corrosive chemicals must be washed out thoroughly with water until every particle has gone. Lids may retract as the burn dries, so the cornea becomes exposed and an ulcer will follow. Snow-blindness is an ultraviolet burn of the cornea.

Rx: chloramphenicol ointment (D.12.1) into the eye twice daily to lubricate the lids and stave off infection. Keep the pupil dilated with two per cent homatropine drops (D.12.3) twice daily to ease painful spasm of the iris. Cover with a pad and bandage so the eyelids won't move over the eyeball and abrade it further.

If the lips, tongue or the nostril hairs are scorched after an explosion, the victim has probably inhaled burning gas and the outcome is poor. The larynx and trachea will swell making the voice husky at first, with croaking later when the airway is blocked. A lung burn usually leads to pneumonia and ultimately to failure of breathing and death.

CHEST AND NECK
If the burn is circumferential a crust, like a breast-plate of armour, may form and restrict breathing.

> Make longitudinal cuts through the full thickness of burned skin to relieve breathing (see below – escharotomy).

HANDS
Burnt hands form nasty contracture deformities unless the hands are kept moving while healing. Cover the whole hand liberally with [sulphadiazine] cream and put it in a plastic bag taped at the wrist. Encourage the victim to exercise his fingers continually to prevent the skin hardening and the fingers becoming stiff. Elevate the hand to reduce swelling. With a bagged hand the victim can do a lot for himself without pain; a mitten over the top protects the bag and looks less distasteful.

Deep burns of the circumference of limbs or fingers harden and the scab may contract like a ring and cut off the blood supply or restrict movement. Check by pin-prick for pain sensation; if absent escharotomy is needed.

This simple surgical procedure, though seemingly drastic, may be
limb-saving. It is especially applicable in order to preserve the fingers
after deep burns round the wrist, which heal with a tight constricting
band. Make a deep knife cut through charred skin along the lateral sides
of the limbs or digits. The wound will spread apart owing to the pressure
within. To be effective the cut must extend beyond the top and bottom of
the eschar down into the unburned zone, which feels pain and may bleed.
If the cuts are adequate, the swollen veins and mottled blue colour of the
skin return to a healthy pink. Where fingers are burned deeply to the tips
all round, it is doubtful if splitting the burn makes much difference.

Finally, do not delay evacuating the victim to hospital, as he will
travel best immediately after the accident, before shock sets in. Do
the best you can in the time available while waiting for rescue.
Reassure the victim that everything is being done to reach help
urgently. Do not brush off his questions, but give a full reply. Let's
hope optimism is warranted.

Heat injury

The body gains heat from its own basal metabolism by exercise, and
from the environment; heat is lost by evaporation from sweating,
conduction and convection.

HEAT EXHAUSTION
Heat exhaustion occurs when metabolic heat production increases
greatly with exertion but thirst does not stimulate adequate drinking
for replacement of fluid. It includes all forms of heat-induced water
and salt depletion, short of heat-stroke. Heat exhaustion can occur
at modest temperatures, $16°$ C ($60°$ F), if exercise is sufficiently
vigorous. The risk is increased on a hot day, in bright sun, high
humidity, calm wind, and by wearing too much heavy, dark,
impermeable clothing. Training to tolerate heat takes at least ten
days.

Look: the victim's temperature, measured rectally, is moderately
raised, $39.5°$ C ($103°$ F) to $42°$ C ($107°$ F). He is very thirsty, sweats
profusely and has a headache and goose-flesh. He is faint, chilled,
nauseated and unsteady. He may become mentally strange,

convulse and fall unconscious, progressing to heat-stroke.

When exercising in the heat, drink water more frequently than thirst dictates, enough to keep the urine clear (4–6 litres daily). When running, drink 250 ml beforehand and every fifteen to thirty minutes throughout the run. An adequate volume of water needs replacing immediately; salt and glucose can be added later. Avoid fancy electrolyte and sugar solutions during activity because they slow absorption of water from the bowel. However, if salt is not replaced later heat-cramps may follow.

Act: cool the victim immediately. Rub ice or snow vigorously on his neck, abdomen, axillae and groin; sprinkle him with cold water to increase evaporation. Immerse his trunk in a stream, but cool his limbs as little as possible because peripheral vessels will constrict, reducing heat-loss.

Rx: 1 litre of five per cent dextrose-saline intravenously over thirty minutes, or as much as he can tolerate by mouth.

HEAT-STROKE

Heat-stroke is a medical emergency and people die from it. The brain function is deranged owing to raised temperature. It can occur at relatively low air temperature if the exercise is vigorous enough and if the air is humid. The risk is increased in someone with a high fever and dehydration.

Look: the victim's rectal temperature is around 41° C (106° F); it may be a degree or two either side of this but heat-stroke cannot be diagnosed by temperature alone. Without warning he may become confused, delirious or comatose. The skin is still sweaty when he collapses but may become hot and dry one to two hours afterwards because of heat damage to the sweat glands.

Act: cool him immediately and thoroughly – it may be life-saving. Only stop cooling when the rectal temperature is 39° C (102° F) because it will drop the rest of the way on its own. With cooling he may start shivering, which can be very painful and may need analgesics.

13 Wounds and poisons

This chapter assumes a medical kit at least as comprehensive as that listed on pages 21–27. Improvising with imagination will have to supplement any missing items.

Superficial wounds

ABRASIONS

Grazes, scrapes and minor burns must be cleaned with plenty of soap and water: 'dilution is the solution to pollution'. Superficial wounds heal best when left open to fresh air allowing them to dry, and form a scab – nature's dressing. Avoid unctions that keep a wound moist; if there are signs of infection an antibiotic by mouth is preferable to antibiotic ointment.

If the wound has to be covered because of oozing, infection, or if the site is unsuitable for exposure, use a sterile gauze dressing held in place with surgical tape or stationery tape.

CUTS

A small sterile dressing (Band-Aid, Elastoplast) should suffice for cover. If the wound edges are cleanly cut, close apposition will give the least scar. Use sterile paper strips (Steri-strips) or butterfly dressings. Paint tincture of benzoin on the surrounding skin to make it tacky and adhesive. Carefully place the strips, alternating the direction of pull of each, so as to bring the edges of the wound together, and keeping the tension equal down the length of the wound. For awkward places – between the fingers, around the ankle – 'Anchor Dressings' conform closely to uneven contours.

BLISTERS

Blisters are usually caused by ill-fitting or stiff boots. Cover a sore 'hot spot' immediately to prevent it rubbing and becoming a fluid-filled blister. Paint the skin around with tincture of benzoin and apply tape directly onto the skin well above and below the rubbed area. Use white surgical tape, silver aluminium duct tape, or moleskin. To take the pressure off a large blister, cut a doughnut from moleskin and place the hole right over the bleb. Leave the tape in place for a week if necessary. Do not burst small blisters; if large, and likely to burst with the rubbing of a boot, clean the skin and puncture the edge in order to release the fluid with a needle, sterilized by holding it in a flame till red hot. Leave the overlying skin in place as a dressing. Clean with soap and water, and dress.

Deep wounds

LACERATIONS

Cut, torn or mangled tissue is best cleaned and left gaping to heal from the bottom of the wound outwards. Closing can be done later if necessary (delayed primary healing) as is done in war wounds. This is much safer than trying to suture wounds out in the wilds where sterility is impossible, and because sutures themselves act as a foreign body in the wound and a focus for infection. For this reason no instructions are given in this book on how to suture, though a simple enough procedure in itself. Nature does a marvellous job with most wounds provided there is no infection; should she fail, a plastic surgeon can tidy up the scar much later.

PUNCTURE WOUNDS

Although tiny on the surface, puncture wounds may have a long track and there's no telling how deeply they penetrate. Beware, those of the chest and abdomen are potential minefields. Seek a surgeon quickly.

GUNSHOT WOUNDS

Leave the bullet or pellets in place unless they are easily extracted.

Bleeding (haemorrhage)

Severe external bleeding will almost always stop with firm pressure directly on the wound, raising the injured part, and resting the victim. Deep internal haemorrhage is a much more serious matter usually needing surgery.

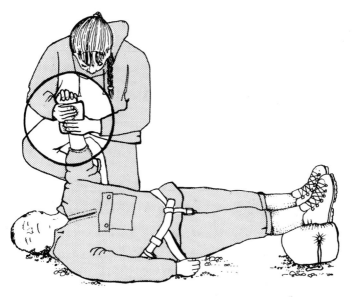

Press and elevate to stop bleeding

An average adult male has about 5½ litres of circulating blood, a female 4½ litres. Each can afford to loose about 1 litre before anaemia and shock are noticed. Loss of more than ⅓ of the total blood volume can kill. Children tolerate blood-loss less well than adults. The difference between bleeding from arteries and veins is academic; severe bleeding whatever its source must be stopped urgently.

Bleeding may halt spontaneously because muscle and elastic tissue in blood vessel walls contract; shed blood forms fibrin clot, but rarely within an undamaged vessel; hidden bleeding in a closed space either closes off vessels in tissue planes between muscles due to the build-up of fluid tension, or bleeding continues unabated into the cavity.

Act: In order to stop bleeding press steadily, firmly and directly on a dressing of absorbent material placed well beyond the edges of the wound and be prepared to keep up pressure for a long time. All bleeding will eventually stop with pressure alone. The dressing should preferably be sterile but do not waste time hunting for a sterile dressing; any reasonably clean material, especially if recently ironed, will do and may save the victim from dying of blood-loss. A doctor can worry about any subsequent infection.

Do not remove soaked dressings; just pack more on top. Clot forms around the mesh of fabric sealing small bleeding vessels and oozing capillaries. If the clot is pulled off bleeding will start again. Cellulose gelatin mesh (Oxycel, Gelfoam) dissolves in the wound and hastens clotting. Wrap absorbent stretchy crêpe (tensor) bandage to keep the wound packing in place. This will splint the area and avoid movement that might restart bleeding.

Forget *pressure points* which are only useful for students of anatomy. Valuable time may be lost while searching for them. Taking a wide, blind suture-needle-bite to close off the wound is not advised because the suture will be a focus for infection, and nerves and other structures in the depths of the wound may be damaged.

Tourniquets can be dangerous because they may obstruct veins without controlling arterial bleeding. They may be tied and then forgotten causing obstruction to blood supply and gangrene of the limb beyond. Pressure may damage nerves. Pain from a tourniquet causes restlessness. In the rare event of a tourniquet being necessary because other methods have failed to control bleeding, for example, traumatic amputation of the hand, release the tourniquet every forty-five minutes, mark a large T on the victim's forehead with a pen or lip-stick, and record the time when it was applied on a label tied round his neck. On the rare occasion when a large artery is severed and bleeding cannot be controlled by pressure alone or a tourniquet, it may be necessary to clamp the ends with a haemostat and tie off the vessel with a suture.

Cleaning – wash the wound with plenty of soap and water to get rid of grease and grime. Plentiful washing gives bacteria less chance to survive and cause infection. Pick out dirt with forceps, but do not scrub because tissue will be further damaged. Antiseptic solutions are no better than soap and water and can cause chemical irritation.

The rescuer's hands should be washed as meticulously as the wound.

Dressings – a sterile dressing should be placed next to the wound. Compressed wound dressings ('shell' dressings) are ideal; tightly packaged women's sanitary napkins are cheap and available. Ironed cloth is sterile; unopened toilet paper or paper tissues are clean, if not sterile. To increase the bulk of a dressing any clean absorbent cloth, like an old shirt, can be slapped on top.

Paraffin gauze squares (Jelonet) are useful for covering oozing wounds; the gauze may be impregnated with antibiotic (Sofratulle). Stretchy clear-plastic kitchen wrap can be applied straight onto a wound or a burn if a closed dressing is required. A mangled limb can be wrapped temporarily in a plastic bag sealed to the skin at both ends with tape.

TETANUS PREVENTION
Anyone planning a trip should be up-to-date with their tetanus immunization; protection lasts for five years. After a wound an anti-tetanus booster dose of 0.5–1.0 ml should be sought from a doctor, who should always ask about previous reactions to anti-tetanus serum, and if in doubt should not give it.

Infection

An inflamed wound looks red, swells, feels hot and throbs painfully. The body is thereby mobilizing its defences of white blood cells, which flow along dilated blood-vessels into the area in order to combat bacteria. An infected wound has pus in it made of gobbled-up bugs and dead tissue which coalesce into a boil or abscess.

LOCALIZED INFECTION: BOIL OR ABSCESS
A tense infected swelling usually comes to a head and forms a white or yellow boil with a soft centre of pus, which may discharge on its own. A red streak, caused by inflamed lymph channels, often leads towards the heart accompanied by local swelling of regional lymph

nodes that drain the infected area: in the groin from the leg, in the armpit from the arm.

Act: heat encourages pus to gather. Soak the area in warm salt water or apply a hot compress (cloth dipped in boiling water and wrung out) six-hourly. Honey, baking soda or glycerine-magnesium-sulphate paste draws out pus hygroscopically.

Where there's pus let it out. When an abscess has a soft centre, indicating liquid pus, lance it to allow the pus to drain. But beware of draining an abscess before it is ripe because it will be painful and produce no pus. A quick stab into the stretched skin over a ripe abscess causes little pain especially if ice or snow is applied for five minutes beforehand. Make the incision deep and long so the hole will not seal over and nullify the good work of drainage. Sudden release of pus under pressure relieves pain instantly. If the hole is deep, pack it with a wick of sterile gauze.

Rx: cephalosporin (D.2.1) as soon as a wound becomes red and inflamed. Avoid antibiotic ointments because they cause sensitivity reactions.

SPREADING INFECTION: CELLULITIS
The skin around a wound looks red and angry, and feels hot and hard owing to swelling. Regional lymph nodes swell. Immobilize the part and elevate it to reduce swelling.

Rx: antibiotics (D.2) i/v if possible, in double dose.

GENERALIZED INFECTION: BLOOD POISONING OR SEPTICAEMIA
High fever and chills in the presence of infection suggest septicaemia – a serious complication which needs urgent medical help.

Rx: antibiotics (D.2) i/v if possible, in double dose and rest.

WOOD SLIVER
Pull the sliver out with forceps or tweezers; but it may be very difficult to find even if judged to be just under the skin. Inject 1 ml of local anaesthetic lignocaine (D.17.1) directly into the area. If the sliver won't come out, soak in hot water and try again but don't damage tissue by persevering. If left alone pus will eventually form

around a sliver, which will extrude with pressure of a developing abscess.

METAL FOREIGN BODY
Leave well alone unless easily removed with tweezers. A broken-off needle fragment may remain inert and harmless for years. Removing it surgically, even with X-ray help, is notoriously difficult.

FISH-HOOK REMOVAL
Push the hook onwards until it pierces the skin again. Cut off the barbed end with pliers, cupping a hand over the cutters to prevent the barb flying into your own eye. Then withdraw the shank of the hook by the way it went in. If pliers are unavailable, hold the eye of the hook down against the skin, loop fishline or string around the hook, and jerk sharply along the plane of the skin surface thereby tearing it out.

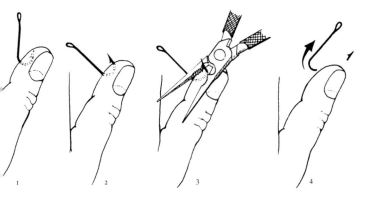

Removing fish-hook

Bruises

Bruises occur when blood is shed under the skin. When the blood breaks down with time the overlying skin turns all the colours of the rainbow.

SUPERFICIAL BRUISES

Black eye – blood collects in the loose tissues around the eye but is enclosed by the margin of the bony orbit. It will subside with ice and time.

Finger-nail blood blister (subungual haematoma) – when a finger-nail is bashed or a boulder drops on a toe, a tense, painful bruise forms at the root of the nail. It turns black, is soggy on pressure and is excruciatingly painful.

  Act: heat an opened metal paper-clip held in forceps or pliers over a stove or flame of a propane lighter (candle flame is not hot enough). When the paper-clip end is red-hot, push it cautiously into the middle of the moon of the nail over the bruise so it burns right through the nail but not into the nail bed. The resulting sizzling smells like a smithy. Old, dark blood spurts out and the sun shines again from the face of the victim, who will be your instant friend, unless you have plunged too deep. Alternatively, drill the base of the nail by rotating a penknife blade or needle.

Deep bruise (haematoma) – a painful swelling can arise from blood pooling in muscle over a point of injury. Rest, elevation and ice may be all that is necessary for it to subside. If the bruise is tense and seems filled with fluid, clean the skin carefully and push the largest available needle into the swelling in order to drain the pooled serum.

Poisons

INHALED GAS

Carbon monoxide is a by-product of most camping stoves and the gas can accumulate in an unventilated tent, especially if sealed with

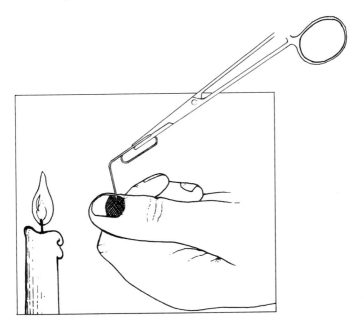

Draining fingernail

snow-cover. In cold weather climbers may camp in their vans, leaving the engine running to heat the cab into which exhaust fumes leak. Carbon monoxide is odourless and a small amount in a tightly-closed space gives little warning of its presence. It can kill rapidly. When found, the victim may be unconscious, very pale and with luck, still alive. A bright-pink skin colour is seen in severe carbon monoxide poisoning.

    Act: remove the victim to fresh air immediately, keep an open airway and give assisted breathing, with oxygen if possible. A vicious headache will develop during recovery and the victim will need analgesics.

SWALLOWED POISONS

Most drugs swallowed accidentally or intentionally must be removed before they are absorbed by the bloodstream. Give an emetic made with milk followed by a strong salty drink and stick a finger down the throat. A stomach wash-out is the most effective way of evacuating poison provided it is done within four hours of swallowing; but it can be dangerous if not done skilfully and preferably with mechanical suction at hand. Corrosives, acids and industrial poisons are best left lying where they are because they will burn the oesophagus if vomited. Dilute them with large volumes of water and/or milk or white of egg.

Act: stomach wash-out only if the person is conscious and can protect his own airway. Lie the victim on his side and pass a well-lubricated tube, at least 1 cm diameter, down the throat into the stomach. Attach a funnel, hold it high, and pour in one litre of water. Lower the funnel below the level of the stomach and let the fluid run out. Repeat until the washings are clear – at least six times.

Drug abuse

Alcohol is the most common drug used, and abused, by climbers; although it loosens social restraints and gives a false sense of bravado, it depresses the nervous system and impairs all reactions. Alcohol compounds the effect of some other drugs.

Strange behaviour, especially after a prolonged, boring spell in camp, may suggest a person is stoned on other drugs. Prevent him from harming himself, maintain an open airway, talk him down in a quiet place and give calm reassurance. Do not leave him unattended until he has emerged from his trip.

COMMONLY ABUSED DRUGS

Hallucinogens – LSD (acid), PCP (angel dust), psilocybin (magic mushrooms) cause hallucinations, agitation and excitement. Pupils are dilated, except with PCP.

Rx: lorazepam (D.5.1).

Narcotics – heroin, morphine, codeine, pethidine, methadone cause seizures, coma and depressed breathing. Pupils are pin-point.

Rx: naloxone (D.1.5) reverses narcotics and restores breathing. Vomiting may need suction. Seizures are controlled with lorazepam preferably given i/v. The victim must be watched closely for twenty-four hours because his breathing may cease, needing resuscitation and more naloxone.

Cannabis group – marijuana, hashish. Eyes are bloodshot, pupils unchanged and the pulse races.

Nervous system depressants 'downers' – barbiturates, diazepam (Valium), chlordiazepoxide (Librium), glutethamide (Doriden), methalqualone (Quaaludes). The depressant effect is increased by alcohol. Severe withdrawal symptoms occur.

Nervous system stimulants 'uppers' – amphetamines (speed), cocaine, anti-obesity drugs. Pupils are dilated but react to light, breathing is shallow, and pulse races. Seizures can occur.

Rx: lorazepam (D.5.1).

Anti-cholinergics – atropine (belladonna), tricyclic anti-depressants, Jimson weed, henbane, mandrake. Pupils are dilated and fixed, pulse races, skin is dry.

Other poisons

FUNGI

Avoid all wild mushrooms unless you are an expert on them. Violent vomiting, diarrhoea, and abdominal cramps come on eight hours after eating the fungi.

Act: give repeated cups of hot tea, an emetic of salty water, Epsom salts and empty the bowel by a soap and water enema.

BOTULISM

Home-canned or bottled food may harbour Clostridium botulinum; seal meat is notorious. Double vision, various muscle paralyses and abdominal discomfort come on after six to twenty-four hours, often in several participants of the same meal.

Act: seek expert help urgently.

Rx: [botulinus antitoxin] 50,000U i/m stat.

Coma

In an unconscious person who has neither story nor sign of head injury, consider other causes of unconsciousness. Look for a Medic-alert bracelet or medallion. But remember that the victim may also have struck his head while falling unconscious.

EPILEPSY

The victim of an epileptic seizure may let out a sudden cry and fall to the ground. He twitches, jerks violently, rolls his eyes, froths at the mouth, bites his tongue and pees in his pants. The seizure usually passes off in a few minutes. He then wakes up, but shortly after will fall into a deep sleep of recovery that can be mistaken for coma.

Act: prevent him from injuring himself. Do not wedge anything between his teeth in order to stop tongue-biting; if the teeth are clenched the victim is conscious enough to be able to safeguard his own airway.

Rx: lorazepam (D.5.1) 1–2 mg i/v would be most effective as an anti-convulsant; by mouth it would act very slowly. If he is a known epileptic on treatment, usually with phenytoin, double the dose for a day and make sure he never forgets to take his pills. Have him checked by a doctor soon.

DIABETES

Diabetics do not produce enough insulin, the hormone that allows the body to burn glucose as fuel for energy. A severe diabetic requires a calculated amount of carbohydrate each day and insulin injections, usually given by himself. Insulin should always be carried by the diabetic because returning to camp may be delayed by a storm or mountaineering problems. If more fuel is expected to be burned, as in a hard day's exercise, temporarily increase carbohydrate intake. Forgetting to do so may lead to either hypoglycaemia (too little sugar) because there is insufficient carbohydrate for the insulin to work on; or diabetic pre-coma (too much sugar) when insulin or oral diabetic medication needs to be increased. Either of these two conditions may cause a slide into coma. Distinguishing which is which is vital because their treatment is contrary.

	Hypoglycaemia	*Diabetic pre-coma*
onset	sudden in healthy	gradual in ill person
appearance	shocked, cool	normal
tongue and skin	moist	dry
breath smell	normal	ketones (acid drops)
urine taste	bitter	sweet
Rx:	glucose	insulin

DRUG OVERDOSE
Alcohol: the smell of the breath gives the story away (except vodka which is odourless).
Narcotics, barbiturates, benzodiazepines and other drug overdoses.
   Act: stomach wash-out (see page 154).

STROKE
Although usually restricted to older people, the young may suffer strokes, especially as a complication of high altitude. The victim first complains of headache, then loses consciousness. The head and eyes turn to one side and he becomes paralysed on the opposite side of the body, partially or completely. Breathing is heavy with snoring and may be periodic (Cheyne-Stokes).
   Act: evacuate urgently as for all the above serious conditions.

HEART ATTACK (myocardial infarction)
Severe chest pain, shock, and rapid breathing occur. Coma is unusual. Heart attack needs pain relief. (See page 32).
   Rx: morphine (D.1.4). Rest and oxygen help cyanosis. If the heart stops start rescue breathing and chest compression. Seek urgent medical help.

Heart and chest

The symptoms and signs of heart and chest illness frequently
overlap. The person may complain of chest pain, irregular
heart-beat, cough, or difficulty and shortness of breathing. Weigh
the history and examination findings in order to reach a diagnosis.
Only conditions reasonably likely to be encountered in the outdoors
are described here.

HISTORY, SYMPTOMS AND SIGNS
Does the person have any past history of heart or chest disease. Is
he now taking any medications? Look for Medic-alert bracelet or
medallion. Allergies? Does he smoke?

Chest pain – ask the nature of the pain and its manner of onset
(sudden or gradual).
– sharp: described as stabbing or knife-like. Pain that is worsened
on inspiration, usually on one side only, and often referred to the
shoulder or abdomen, probably arises from the lung surface
(pleurisy). Pain very sharply localized to one tender rib may be due
to fracture. Chest wall pain is accentuated by movement.
– dull: also described as gripping, vice-like, crushing, constricting.
Angina typically is pain, pressure or tightness in the centre or left
side of the chest, or deep behind the sternum, possibly referred to
the shoulder or arms or up into the neck or jaw, usually in someone
with known heart disease. It comes on with exertion and is relieved
by rest. Heart attack (myocardial infarction) may be associated with
shortness of breath and sweaty, nauseating shock.

Pulse – rapid and regular: may be due to paroxysmal atrial
tachycardia (PAT) which can occur in healthy people and may
cause an uncomfortable feeling behind the sternum, like butterflies,
which engenders anxiety but usually needs no treatment. On rare
occasions it may be serious and cause shock. Tachycardia may be
caused by fever or lack of oxygen (hypoxia) especially at altitude.
– rapid and irregular: suggests heart disease; if combined with chest
pain think of myocardial infarction.

– slow (bradycardia): many athletes run a pulse of less than fifty beats per minute. It can also occur in heart-block from myocardial infarction.

Cough – Sudden, violent coughing and choking may be due to an inhaled foreign body. A dry cough occurs in early bronchitis; later yellow or green sputum appears. Bright-red or rusty blood-flecked sputum suggests pneumonia, which is often accompanied by fever and rigors. Pulmonary oedema causes a dry cough with no sputum, less commonly a moist cough with pink, frothy sputum. Cough at altitude can be due to the dry air; it is very irritating and may be so violent as to break a rib.

Shortness of breath (dyspnoea) – upper airway obstruction may be accompanied by noisy, croupy, whooping stridor worse during inspiration.
– air or fluid in the pleural cavity: air arises from collapse of lung (pneumothorax – spontaneous or traumatic), fluid comes from an effusion possibly after pneumonia.
– stiffness of the lung because of congestion, consolidation (pneumonia) or oedema due to heart failure caused by myocardial infarction: often accompanied by dyspnoea on lying down and swelling of the ankles.

Wheeze – noisy wheezing and dyspnoea, especially during expiration and sometimes with cyanosis, suggests asthma or bronchitis. An asthma attack may be provoked by contact with an allergen, for example, pollen, dust, feathers, animal fur or certain foods. Other causes are chest infection (bronchitis or pneumonia) or emotional upset.

Sputum – if the spit is thick yellow or green, chest infection is present and an antibiotic is needed.

Exam: look, feel, listen

Heart
Look: for swelling of the ankles which pits on finger pressure and shows the imprint of sock elastic, indicating heart failure.

Look for raised jugular venous pressure indicating right heart failure. Look for the colour and nutrition of the skin of the extremities.

Cyanosis – a bluish colour of the skin and lips should be sought in full daylight because it can be missed in the poor lighting of a coloured tent. Weather-beaten, sun-tanned skin may disguise cyanosis. It occurs in two forms.
– peripheral: seen best in the beds of the finger-nails and the lips, due to sluggish flow of cold blood. The colour returns to normal pink on warming. The tongue remains pink. Peripheral cyanosis occurs in shock when the blood-pressure falls due to circulatory failure.
– central: the tongue, lips, and mucous membranes inside the mouth are blue and do not turn pink on re-warming.

Central cyanosis indicates serious disturbance of heart and lung function because of either inadequate ventilation, uneven distribution of blood, decreased diffusion of oxygen, or abnormal shunting of blood within the chambers of the heart. It is common at high altitude because of diminished oxygen (hypoxia) and excessive red blood cell production (polycythemia). To judge cyanosis at altitude compare a healthy climber with the sick person. Central cyanosis disappears on breathing 100 per cent oxygen for ten minutes.

Feel: the pulse and gauge the blood-pressure (or measure it with a sphygmomanometer). Light finger-touch can tell whether the pulse is full and bounding, or weak and thready.

Feel the apex beat, which shows an enlarged heart if displaced to the left. Feel the peripheral pulses; femoral, posterior tibial and dorsalis pedis, to assess the peripheral circulation.

Listen: to the heart sounds, preferably with a stethoscope, if not, with an ear placed against the victim's chest. Abnormal rhythms may be more easily detected with the ear than the finger. Only an experienced, trained ear can interpret abnormal heart sounds.

Chest

Look: at the chest, bared from chin to belly-button. Note the rate, depth and rhythm of chest movements – more can be seen by standing 2 m back than by peering from close proximity. One side of the chest may move less well than the other in pneumonia or collapsed lung (pneumothorax). Look at the accessory muscles that strain when breathing is laboured: flared nostrils, gasping mouth, taut neck muscles, and indrawn intercostal muscles between the ribs.

Feel: by placing hands lightly against the sides of his chest with fingers pointing towards his armpits. Unequal movement can be felt more easily on deep breathing.

Percussion of the chest, thumping with one finger against a finger of the other hand placed against the chest, – is hard to interpret even for a trained physician.

Listen: to both sides of the chest, front and back, from top to bottom, and have the victim breathe gently through his mouth. Air entry should be equal on both sides and can be noted by moving an ear from one side to the other. Breath sounds should be clear and unrestricted. Wheeze is easily picked up on expiration. Other sounds of fluid in the air passages may be heard as rough crackling, like crumpling paper, or fine crackling, like rubbing hair between fingers in front of the ear (crepitations). At high altitude think of pulmonary oedema.

Asthma, bronchitis, and pneumonia may be difficult to distinguish.

ASTHMA

Asthma is associated with hay fever and eczema. It may be precipitated by acute infection, aspirin, specific allergens (pollens, dust), exertion, excitement and cold air. Spasm of the bronchi causes wheezing, especially on expiration, a tight chest and dry cough which later produces sputum when infection is present. Feel the pulse racing, and listen for crackles and expiratory wheeze with an ear on the back of the victim's chest.

Rx: salbutamol (D.8.1) puffer; if it does not settle a course of prednisone (D.4.1). In a severe asthmatic attack Rx: adrenaline (D.7.2).

Status Asthmaticus: is an attack of asthma lasting more than twenty-four hours. The symptoms are as above, together with shortness of breath and cyanosis. The victim becomes drowsy, and can rapidly slide into shock and die.

Rx: salbutamol (D.8.1), prednisone (D.4.1).

BRONCHITIS

Infection of the upper respiratory tract, the common cold, laryngitis, or pharyngitis are all commonly caused by viruses and frequently develop a superimposed secondary bacterial infection. Wheeze, fever and cough with yellow or green spit are produced. Crackles can be heard at the back of the chest.

PNEUMONIA

Pneumonia, which may be bacterial or viral, causes cough with rusty or bloody sputum, fever and rigors. Breathing is rapid and painful owing to pleurisy.

Act: *Secretions:* inhale steam from a kettle or billy of boiling water, which can also be poured onto a teaspoonful of tincture of benzoin put in an old tin. A towel over the head makes a tent in order to concentrate the steam, but beware of scalding. Sip a cup of boiling water with one tablespoon of baking soda and one tablespoon of salt added. Thump the chest with the person lying on alternating sides and head tipped down.

Bronchial relaxant: Rx: salbutamol (D.8.1) in a mild attack of bronchospasm.

Cough suppressant: Rx: codeine (D.1.3) at night dampens cough to allow sleep, but should not be used by day. Expectorant cough mixtures are popular but their effect is not proven.

Antibiotics: Rx: cephalosporin (D.2.1) or co-trimoxazole (D.2.2) for
at least a week if the sputum is yellow or green, or if there is a fever.
Analgesics: Rx: morphine (D.1.4) may be needed for severe
pleuritic pain in order to allow full breathing, but be prepared to
reverse with naloxone (D.1.5).
Steroids: Rx: dexamethasone (D.4.2) i/v, or a short course of
prednisone (D.4.1) by mouth, should be used in people who have
been on steroids before, and may help in asthma.
Oxygen: relieves breathlessness and cyanosis.

ALLERGY

The body responds to the introduction of foreign substances
(antigens) by forming protein antibodies in the blood. An excessive
stimulus may cause an allergic reaction, or hypersensitivity, owing
to release of histamine. For example, some people are sensitive to
penicillin and break out in a rash; severe reactions result in
life-threatening anaphylactic shock. Common allergies result from
contact with pollens and moulds, house dust and house-mites,
animal dandruff and hair, and certain foods such as shellfish and
chocolate. The symptoms, uncomfortable but not dangerous, are of
asthma, hay fever (with running nose and eyes), or hives on the skin
with itchy raised weals.

Rx: antihistamine (D.3) allays itching and speeds the
disappearance of symptoms.

ANAPHYLAXIS

Immediate, severe, shock-like and often fatal reactions follow
contact with an antigen: a bee or wasp sting; a drug (especially
penicillin and aspirin); injection of immune serum (tetanus
antiserum and snake antivenom) or, rarely, of vaccines. The
symptoms are of apprehension and shock, choking, wheezy asthma
with cough and cyanosis. Blotchy skin weals develop all over the
body; untreated, the victim may lose consciousness, convulse and
die within five to ten minutes.

People with known sensitivity to bee or wasp stings should carry a
first-aid kit with a preloaded syringe of adrenaline.

Rx: adrenaline (D.7.2) 0.3 – 1.0 ml of 1:1000 i/m or s/c repeated in the first five to ten minutes. Keep the victim's airway open and place him in the draining position. Put up i/v fluids. [Hydrocortisone] 100–250 mg i/v in the first thirty minutes followed by a course of prednisone orally.

Gut

INDIGESTION

Stomach gas may cause a bloated, dyspeptic feeling behind the lower end of the breast-bone (sternum), or in the upper abdomen (epigastrium) and is often relieved by a hearty belch. The discomfort, colloquially known as heart-burn, may be so severe as to mimic the chest pain of a heart attack and many people have spent the night in intensive care wired up to electronic monitors until cured by a glass of milk and a dose of antacid white medicine. Farting may also be a social problem, especially at high altitude. One serious American wilderness medicine text gives the advice

> one should not attempt to ignite rectal gas or direct a stream of gas into a campfire. Backflashes and minor burns are a real risk.

Avoid heavy meals but do not let the stomach lie empty for long periods because stomach acid starts to gnaw away at the lining, which is how ulcers start. Every two hours eat a biscuit with a glass of milk, which coats the stomach and gives the natural hydrochloric acid something to work on. Aspirin is very irritating, and in a sensitive person one tablet may spark off a significant bleed (haematemesis). Avoid fried food, fats, spices, nicotine, coffee and alcohol, all of which stimulate gastric acid production. What joys are there left in life?

Rx: aluminium hydroxide (D.9.1), the base of a multitude of antacids; the liquid form gives quickest relief. but tablets are more convenient for the pocket and can be bought across the counter in many proprietary forms.

Simple indigestion may be difficult to distinguish from acid regurgitation, peptic ulcer and gall-bladder disease. In every instance when far from help treat as above, and if the symptoms persist seek a doctor for a proper diagnosis.

ACID REGURGITATION

The lining of the gullet (oesophagus) does not take kindly to stomach acid; regurgitating water-brash causes burning pain behind the sternum. This also occurs when a portion of the upper stomach slides through a gap in the diaphragm into the chest (hiatus hernia). Discomfort is worst when lying flat and may cause vomiting; it is relieved by sleeping propped-up and taking the precautions described above.

PEPTIC ULCER

Gastric or duodenal ulcers cause gnawing pain in the pit of the stomach coming on a couple of hours after meals, and only partially relieved by indigestion treatment. A history may reveal that the ulcer has been lying dormant for years, but then may flare up under stress or unaccustomed eating and living conditions. The danger is of a sudden, torrential, life-threatening bleed (haematemesis) or perforation (peritonitis).

Rx: aluminium hydroxide (D.9.1), famotidine (D.9.2) for at least a month even if symptoms subside.

GALL-BLADDER DISEASE

Mild gall-bladder inflammation (cholecystitis) causes indigestion and constant pain under the right rib margin which is also felt in the right shoulder tip and/or through to the back under the right shoulder blade. Jaundice, seen as yellow whites of the eyes and a tinge to the skin, may be present with pale, putty-like stools and mahogany-dark urine. Food is nauseating.

A severe gall-bladder attack owing to a gallstone lodged in the duct causes excruciating colic, the victim is very sick and needs urgent surgical help.

Rx: cephalosporin (D.2.1) may resolve cholecystitis.

JAUNDICE

Infectious hepatitis is the most likely cause of jaundice in climbers. The victim feels rotten for about a week before the whites of the eyes turn yellow, and the skin begins to itch, eventually going yellow. Pain is usually absent. He may feel better once jaundice appears. Full recovery may take months and may be prolonged if rest, which is the only treatment, is curtailed.

Several infectious diseases, especially those caused by viruses, have a similar prodrome of malaise before the illness becomes manifest, for example, influenza, and glandular fever (mononucleosis).

CONSTIPATION

Not drinking enough is the commonest cause of this miserable state. Dehydrated foods make it worse and contribute to noisome gas. Eat a preventive diet of bran, cereal roughage and fruit. If this fails use mineral oil, bisacodyl laxative (D.9.4), or a soap and water enema, in that order. Dehydration can turn the stools to concrete and ruin a trip (and may even require manual removal with a well-greased finger).

DIARRHOEA
(see page 234)

VOMITING

A stomach upset from dietary indiscretion or food poisoning may cause a short burst of vomiting, which usually settles in a day by stopping eating and only taking sips of fluid. If vomiting persists suspect some more serious intra-abdominal mischief and seek medical help.

Skin problems

ECZEMA (Dermatitis)
Associated with allergies and contact with certain drugs, nickel and cosmetics.

Rx: betamethasone (D.11.1) ointment.

IMPETIGO

A superficial infection of the skin usually with staphylococcus. A vesicle becomes a pustule that forms characteristic yellow crusty scabs usually on the face.

Rx: cephalosporin (D.2.1) by mouth.

TINEA

A fungal infection causing athlete's foot and dhobie itch of the crotch. A red, silver-scaly rash that is very irritating.

Rx: clotrimazole (D.11.2) antifungal cream.

SCABIES

This condition is caused by a mite that thrives in bedding and unclean clothing. It burrows forming a pin-head vesicle, which becomes scratched as it is maddeningly irritating especially when warm in bed.

Rx: [benzyl benzoate] applied from neck to toes, and repeated in five days.

LICE AND NITS

They lay eggs on hair shafts and cause wild itching.

Rx: [benzyl benzoate.]

Psychological problems

Many psychological problems are alleviated by the peace of the hills. For this very reason many of us choose them as our escape from worldly cares. However when anxiety is manifest we must be able to distinguish panic from psychosis.

PANIC

Under arduous conditions or during a difficult ascent a climber may lose his nerve and become frightened, agitated and acutely anxious. Although rational, he is paralysed with fear and becomes ineffective.

Act: talk the person down with calm reassurance; anger will only provoke him. If still out of control when back at camp Rx:

lorazepam (D.5.1). Wait until next morning to see if he returns to normal after a good sleep; if so, the condition is panic and not psychosis, which would take much longer to settle. The person will probably be deeply ashamed of the episode, so encourage him to talk and get it off his chest. Such emotions might be the lot of any of us on another occasion so much empathy is needed.

PSYCHOSIS

Madness, as distinct from panic, does not usually start out of the blue without some previous warning of mental imbalance. In selecting a climbing team be wary of someone with a record of strange behaviour; intuitive feelings may be right. The person may lose touch with reality and have bizarre hallucinations. He feels that other people are ganging up on him and he may appear so convincing that you begin to wonder who is crazy, you or he. He tends to over-react to normal situations and may be violent and excited, or passive and withdrawn. Once the acute phase of a psychotic episode has passed, a more drawn-out depression sets in when the person is most likely to attempt suicide.

Act: heavy sedation with Rx: lorazepam (D.5.1) will quieten the person; if he becomes violent try to prevent him from injuring himself and others. Forcible restraint may only worsen the situation making him more excited, but may be needed in the last resort.

15 Eyes

The eyeball horrifies some people and few can even bring themselves to inspect it closely. Only careful observation, preferably with magnification, will allow intelligent treatment.

Ask: the victim to read newsprint of various sizes from normal reading distance, with glasses if he usually wears them and using each eye separately. Was each eye perfect before the present problem arose? Recording the vision now will help in following progress.

Is the eye painful? Scratches of the window of the eye (cornea) commonly give the sensation of a foreign body; infection of the conjunctiva (the thin, loose, transparent membrane over the white sclera of the eye) feels like grit or sand in the eyes.

Are there persistent flashes of light, blurred patches in the vision, or strange visual sensations? All are abnormal.

Look: at the eye with a flashlight and a magnifying glass, a loupe or a camera lens. A drop of local anaesthetic amethocaine (D.12.4) placed in the gutter of the lid (fornix) makes the task easier because the victim will relax his tightly screwed up eyes. It takes less than a minute to act.

Lids – pull down the lower lid to look for a foreign body in the fornix and then evert the upper lid as this is a common place for uninvited matter to lodge. When anaesthetized sweep a match-stick, with cotton wool wound onto the tip, along both upper and lower fornices. If nothing appears, leave some eye ointment in the lower fornix and a foreign body may eventually float out.

Lashes – inturned lashes scratch the cornea like barbs and are the source of much discomfort. Pluck them out with tweezers.

Conjunctiva – red and swollen conjunctiva denotes inflammation or infection, which causes aversion to bright light, tearing and a yellow discharge.

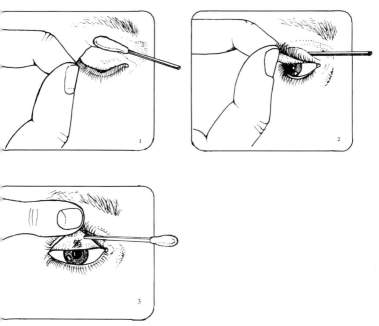

Everting eyelid

Cornea – is normally clear and shiny. If fluorescein dye on a dampened paper strip is touched against the inner aspect of the lower lid, any breach in the corneal surface caused by abrasions, ulcers or foreign bodies shows up as a bright-green stain.

Pupil – is normally circular and constricts when light is shone into it; an eccentric pupil suggests problems in the anterior chamber of the eye.

Act: dark glasses or a pirate's patch keep out light that is painful. A firm bandage over several eye-pads gives pressure on the lids and stops blinking which irritates the cornea. An eye-pad held on with sticky tape alone does not provide enough pressure to keep the lids closed and becomes loose, damp and uncomfortable.

Tea: contains tannic acid which is astringent, soothing, cheap, available and there is no limit to how often it can be instilled. For an uncomfortable, scratchy, painful eye squeeze cold tea from a moist tea bag (Darjeeling or Earl Grey are equally effective) into the lower fornix. If there is infection with pussy discharge use an antibiotic (D.12.1), but these are much over-prescribed; they all have chemical bases which sting and cause irritation that can compound an existing problem.

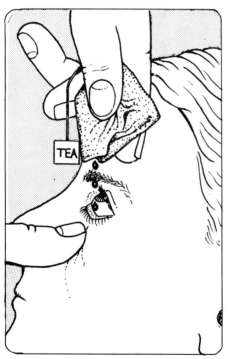

Eye drops

Local anaesthetic: amethocaine (D.12.4) freezes the eye allowing foreign bodies to be removed. Cover the eye afterwards until sensation returns. Local anaesthetic delays healing so must not be used over a long period to relieve pain, but it could be life-saving in allowing a snow-blind climber to return to a lower camp.

Pupil dilator (mydriatic): homatropine 2 per cent (D.12.3) dilates the pupil if instilled twice daily, and relieves painful spasm that follows abrasion or injury of the cornea. It blurs vision making the eye sensitive to light, so use dark glasses or a patch. Homatropine is short-acting, lasting for twenty-four hours after the last drop, unlike atropine which dilates the pupil for a couple of weeks. The remote chance of inducing glaucoma should not discourage the use of a short-acting mydriatic; besides relieving pain it also offers a better view of the back of the eye for someone with the skill to use an ophthalmoscope. However, it should not be used in the presence of a head injury because it confuses the pupil signs of cerebral compression, or in hyphaema when blood cells may block the drainage angle and cause glaucoma.

Antibiotic: chloramphenicol (D.12.1). Antiseptics have no place, and patent remedies containing mercury (Golden Eye ointment) may cause sensitivity reactions. When there is danger of infection, an ulcer or if pus is present, use antibiotics. Ointment stays around the eye and need only be put in twice a day, but it feels gooey and fogs the vision. Drops must be instilled at least six-hourly.

Steroid: dexamethasone (D.12.2) has a magical effect on many red eyes but should be avoided unless in skilled hands because it delays healing and if used in herpes virus infection, may rot the cornea.

Infection and inflammation (painful red eye(s))

INFECTION

Conjunctivitis – usually both eyes feel gritty as though sand is in them; they look red, may water and discharge, and they resent bright light (photophobia). The vision is unaffected.
   Rx: antibiotic (D.12.1), dark glasses.

Corneal ulcer – fluorescein shows up a stain usually central and circular. Vision will be interrupted if the ulcer lies on the visual axis in the centre of the cornea. Corneal ulcers are usually caused by bacteria, may take one to two weeks to heal, and can scar permanently.

Rx: mydriatic (D.12.3), antibiotic (D.12.1), dark glasses.

Herpes simplex – a mature herpetic corneal ulcer has squiggly, branching arms (dendrites), which stain with fluorescein. Look for 'kissing', or cold sores on the lips which give away the diagnosis. Herpes is a virus, hard to diagnose without magnification, and difficult to treat. If someone has had herpes infection before and gets a red eye, presume it is herpes again.

Rx: mydriatic (D.12.3), [arabinase (Viroptic)] two-hourly for three days, then six-hourly for a week, dark glasses.

INFLAMMATION

Iritis – usually a single eye becomes red, painful, photophobic and the vision is blurred. The pupil may be stuck to the lens; it appears irregular and is immobile in response to light. Iritis is difficult to diagnose without huge magnification. A history of previous attacks should arouse suspicion.

Rx: mydriatic (D.12.3), steroid (D.12.2), dark glasses.

Contact lens keratitis – contact lenses scratch the cornea causing painful inflammation. If the lens is left out the cornea usually heals in twenty-four to forty-eight hours. Tea will soothe meanwhile. To remove a soft contact lens, moisten the tip of the index finger, hold the lids open with the other hand, look down, and pinch it off with finger and thumb.

Eyelid cysts and styes – occur as uncomfortable, red, swollen lumps on the lid margins, sometimes with a core of pus.

Act: try to pull out any lash that may appear to arise from the centre of the lump. Apply heat by winding cloth round a wooden stick, dipping it in boiling water and holding it as close to the eye as

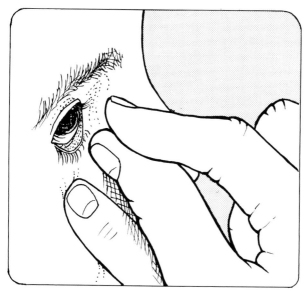

Removing contact lens

possible without scalding the lid. The heat will soothe, and the cyst/stye may come to a head and burst. Antibiotics locally are to no avail.

Injuries

CLOSED INJURY (non-penetrating)

Subconjunctival haemorrhage – a mild bang on the eye, or even rubbing it during sleep, can spill a single drop of blood that spreads out under the loose sheet of conjunctiva. The eye goes a horrifying scarlet and will change through all the colours of the rainbow and fade within three weeks. It is of no sinister import provided the posterior limit of the blood is visible by turning the eye towards the

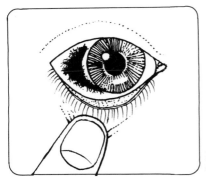

Eye injury:
subconjunctival haemorrhage

nose; if, in a serious injury with bruised and black eyes, no posterior
limit is visible suspect bleeding from the brain – a very serious sign.

Corneal abrasion – caused, for example, by inturned eyelashes, a
brush with a twig or pine needle, or a flying wood chip. The eye is
very painful for twenty-four to forty-eight hours by which time most
abrasions are healed. If pain persists more than two days consider
an ulcer or infection.

   Act: pluck out an inturned lash for instant relief. If the cause is
otherwise, Rx: tea, if infection is suspected Rx: mydriatic (D.12.3),
antibiotic drops (D.12.1), analgesic (D.1), dark glasses.

Foreign body – a speck of dirt or metal embedded in the cornea can
often be seen with the naked eye. Sometimes it is lodged in the
fornix of the upper or lower lid, or is stuck to the underside of the
upper lid where it scratches with every blink.

   Act: lie the person down to avoid fainting; then wash the eye with
plenty of water. Rx: local anaesthetic (D.12.4) two drops. Try to
wipe the speck away with a folded corner of tissue. If it won't
budge, use a pushing motion with the end of a matchstick
approaching cautiously from the side to avoid digging into the
cornea.

   Rx: mydriatic (D.12.3), tea; only use antibiotic (D.12.1) if
infection is evident.

Even if a metal foreign body is removed, residual iron pigment will subsequently form a ring of rust where the metal lay in contact with the cornea. A rust ring must be removed later by an eye specialist. Observe for perforation (see below).

BURNS – when the face is burned the lids take the brunt of the damage because blinking usually occurs before flame touches the cornea. Corneal burns may be caused by fire sparks, ultraviolet light and chemicals.

Ultraviolet burn (Snow blindness): sun reflects strongly off snow and light-coloured rocks; its rays penetrate hazy cloud and become more powerful with altitude. The resulting ultraviolet burn of the cornea causes intensely painful inflammation so the eyes are screwed up tightly. About six hours after burning, swelling of the conjunctiva and blistering of the cornea prevent the victim from seeing and he becomes temporarily blind and has to be led or

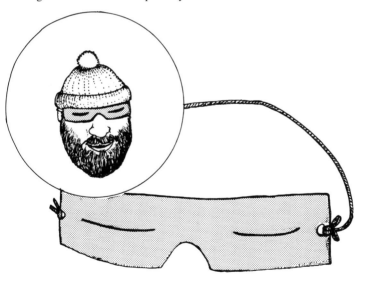

Snow goggles

carried to a lower camp on the mountain, with all the attendant risks.

Act: snow-blindness is prevented by wearing goggles or dark glasses with side-shields to exclude glare. In emergency cut horizontal slits in a piece of cardboard, or duct-tape doubled on itself, and tie it round the head with a piece of string, like Eskimo snow-goggles.

Rx: analgesics (D.1) and tea; local anaesthetic drops (D.12.4) will relieve pain and spasm long enough for the victim to reach camp unaided and so may be life-saving. Do not use anaesthetic drops for prolonged pain relief afterwards. After reaching safety both eyes are then treated like severe corneal abrasions.

Chemical burns: caused by battery acid, or lime.

Act: wash the eye immediately and repeatedly with plenty of water for at least five minutes and remove any lumps of chemical.

Rx: mydriatic (D.12.3), analgesic (D.1), plus washing with bicarbonate of soda (baking soda) for acid burns, which usually heal quickly; or milk or vinegar for alkali burns, the consequences of which are often severe.

BRUISING – after a blow on the globe of the eye the injury may be in the *anterior chamber*, in front of the pupil, called a hyphaema. Blood may completely fill the chamber and obscure vision. After a few hours it settles forming a crescent at the bottom of the chamber. If the victim does not rest completely there is danger of more bleeding and a serious threat to vision.

Act: complete rest with one eye patched, for four to five days if possible.

Rx: analgesics and a sedative, lorazepam (D.5.1), to make lying still easier. Do not dilate the pupil because blood may block off the drainage angle and cause glaucoma. Use tea only. If the eye remains inflamed after four days start steroid drops (D.12.2) six-hourly.

Alternatively the injury may be in the *posterior chamber*, only visible with an ophthalmoscope.

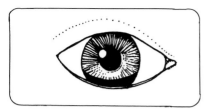

Eye injury: hyphaema

Bleeding into the vitreous jelly: vision is very blurred and no red background is visible with an ophthalmoscope, just a black reflection.
Retinal detachment: a shadow may appear like a curtain falling across the vision, wavy shadows of matter floats around in the vitreous and there may be a sensation of flashing lights.

   Act: both conditions need an eye surgeon. Patch the eye meanwhile, and rest as much as possible.
High Altitude Retinal Haemorrhage (HARH): (see page 220).

OPEN INJURY (penetrating)

Infection and disorganization of the interior of the eye are hazards of penetrating injury. A wound may be seen across the cornea (less commonly the white sclera) but often the wound is tiny and seals over disguising the mischief. Vision is reduced and the eye is red. The iris lies close against the back of the cornea. The pupil may be irregular and pear-shaped because part of the iris gets caught in the

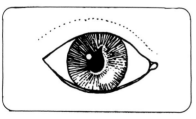

Eye injury: pear shaped pupil

wound. To test for anterior chamber fluid touch a fluorescein paper strip on the upper part of the eye and observe closely for a streak of fluorescence dribbling down where eye fluid and dye mix.

Act: penetrating injuries are very serious and warrant an eye surgeon's urgent attention. Sympathetic inflammation can occur within two weeks in the opposite uninjured eye leading to blindness.

Rx: double dose of antibiotic cephalosporin (D.2.1) by mouth, analgesics (D.1) and dark glasses.

EYELID INJURY

Always check the globe of the eye for associated injury. Eyelid repair requires great surgical skill in order to restore accurately the windscreen-wiper mechanism. Beware an injury in the corner of the eye near the nose where the tiny tear ducts may have been torn; they need speedy repair.

Rx: antibiotic drops (D.12.1), pain-killers and patch meanwhile.

FACIAL FRACTURE

The bony ring around the orbit may be disrupted. The eyeball sinks causing double vision (diplopia). The cheek is flattened and tender and sometimes a step may be felt in the smooth lower rim of the orbit by running a finger along the skin.

Act: a pirate's patch eliminates diplopia until a surgeon can be reached.

16   Ears, nose, throat and teeth

Ears

ACUTE EAR INFECTION (otitis media)
Searing pain develops in the affected ear, usually with high fever.
Hearing is dulled. Fluid under pressure in the middle-ear may result
in rupture of the ear-drum and discharge of clear fluid. Earache may
also be caused by a faulty upper wisdom tooth.

   Act: a light cotton-wool plug in the outer-ear keeps out cold,
which aggravates pain. Warm olive oil dropped into the ear, and
placing the ear against a hot water-bottle, is soothing.

   Rx: cephalosporin (D.2.1).

FOREIGN BODY
Small round objects and insects may lodge in the outer-ear. Wax is
wafted towards the outside by hairs in the ear canal.

   Act: pull back the earlobe in order to straighten the canal and to
give a clear view in as far as the drum. Lubricate the ear passage
with a couple of drops of liquid paraffin or olive oil. Turn the head
on one side and shake vigorously. Gently flush the ear with clean,
warm water using a syringe; 5–10 irrigations should allow the
foreign matter to slide out. Do not dig for wax or poke around with
match-sticks because the ear-drum may be damaged. If a foreign
body is seen in the canal try to pick it out with tweezers or a wire
loop manoeuvred past it and then withdrawn.

EUSTACHIAN TUBE BLOCKAGE
When the tube leading from the back of the throat to the middle-ear
is blocked by swelling owing to a throat infection, or by sudden
change in pressure such as altitude change in aeroplanes, hearing is
dulled and the person feels like yawning to relieve the block.

   Act: yawn, swallow hard, or blow out against a closed nose,
mouth and throat. Blockage usually clears in its own time. If it is
imperative to fly when suffering from a cold, before take-off and
landing chew gum.

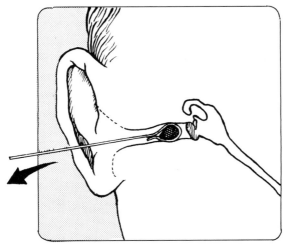

Foreign body in ear

Rx: ephedrine (D.14.1) decongestant nose-drops and steam inhalation six-hourly.

LABYRINTHITIS

Virus infection in the middle-ear, often following a cold, upsets the balance making the person feel unsteady, nauseated and utterly miserable.

Act: rest and Rx: antihistamine (D.3) helps a little; it is sedative, which may be an asset. Time is the healer but it may take six weeks.

MENIÈRE'S DISEASE

Severe vertigo induces falling to the ground, nausea, vomiting and profuse sweating, followed by deafness and ringing in the ears – a most unpleasant combination.

Act: reassure the person it will pass, and restrict salt.

Rx: antihistamines (D.3).

Mouth

MOUTH ULCERS
Canker sores – are painful and irritating.

Traumatic ulcers – are caused by a tooth rubbing the inside of the cheek.
   Act: mouth washes of salt or baking soda. Gentian violet paint made from crystals is mucky to use but heals mucosal surfaces like the mouth.

Herpes simplex – sores frequently accompany colds, especially at high altitude. They are contagious and occur on the lips, inside the nostrils, and rarely, though much publicized, on the genitals. They form blisters which crust, scab and heal after two to three weeks.
   Act: wash all eating irons, cups and utensils carefully. Keep the blisters dry by dabbing with alcohol, and refrain from kissing.

Nose

COMMON COLD
Colds are caused by viruses but are one of the commonest nuisances that affect climbers. Runny nose, sore throat and fever usually clear within a week. Antibiotics have no effect on viruses and should not be used.
   Act: avoid contagion by sleeping head-to-toe in a well-ventilated tent. Use steam inhalation with tincture of benzoin, gargle with 1 tsp of salt in 1 litre of water. Garlic cloves, chilli peppers, mustard plasters or horse radish may help; don't waste money, space or energy carrying extra vitamins but give zinc tablets a try.
   Rx: paracetamol (D.1.1), ephedrine (D.14.1) nose-drops. A cold that settles on the chest may lead to bronchitis; yellow or green spit indicates pus from a secondary bacterial infection. Rx: antibiotic (D.2).

SINUSITIS

Infection of the air sinuses around the face produces yellow or green snot. Severe headache is felt over the forehead or behind the eyes, and pain and tenderness are felt over the cheek or brow overlying the sinuses, or in the upper teeth. Frontal sinusitis may spread back to the brain causing meningitis, but this is rare.

Act: inhale steam in order to encourage drainage by liquefying snot, and shrinking the swollen mucosal lining of the air passages.

Rx: decongestants (D.14.1), antibiotics (D.2).

HAY FEVER (allergic rhinitis)

Watery nasal discharge, itchy eyes and nose, and sneezing are signs of nasal congestion.

Rx: decongestant (D.14.1), antihistamine (D.3).

NOSEBLEED (epistaxis)

Bleeding usually stops on its own after a few minutes with ice and pressure alone, but occasionally it may be so uncontrollable as to threaten life. Bleeding is never a safety-valve, as folklore would have it, but it may indicate high blood-pressure. Bleeding arises from the septum between the nostrils or high in the nose, well out of sight.

Act: sit the person up, leaning slightly forward with the head bowed. Encourage him to blow clots out of his nostrils, which do nothing to stop further bleeding and just dam up blood that trickles down the back of the throat into the stomach and will make him vomit. Identify from which side the blood is coming. Place a cold compress, preferably of ice or snow wrapped in a damp cloth, across the bridge of the nose. Squeeze the nostrils for twenty minutes below where the bone and soft nose cartilage join. Discourage breathing through the nose, picking at clots, blowing the nose, or sneezing, for twenty-four hours. If the air is very dry, as at altitude or in severe cold, apply vaseline inside the affected nostril once the bleeding has stopped.

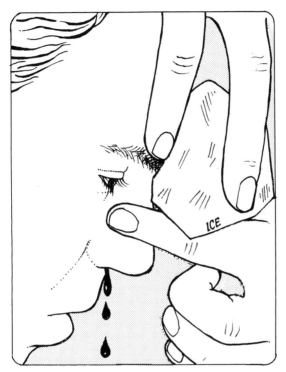

Stopping nosebleed

If bleeding persists push a gauze pack soaked in adrenaline (D.7.2) or ephedrine (D.14.1) as high as possible up the offending nostril and leave it there for twenty-four to forty-eight hours. If bleeding restarts on removing the gauze, repack the nostril. A mountainside is no place for the amateur to try packing the post-nasal space via the mouth; a manoeuvre fraught with hazard.

Packing the post-nasal space should only be done by someone with the appropriate skill. Sew three long strings of thread securely through a rolled gauze square. Pass a soft rubber catheter (or a Foley catheter, and blow up the balloon later) through the bleeding nostril, past the pharynx and out through the mouth. Tie two of the strings to the catheter tip and draw them back through the nose. Guide the pack up behind the uvula while pulling on the strings. Anchor the strings by tying them over a rolled gauze up against the nostril. Pull the third string out of the mouth and tape it to the face in order to pull on later in order to remove the pack. Leave the pack in not longer than four days.

BROKEN NOSE

An isolated fracture and the associated black eyes mar beauty; if associated with other facial fractures the injury is more significant and means a serious head injury.

Act: ice reduces the swelling until a surgeon can deal with the fracture.

Throat

SORE THROAT

Virus infection, the commonest form of sore throat, turns the throat fiery red. There is no pus and the infection does not respond to antibiotics.

Act: gargle with aspirin dissolved in warm water and then swallow the gargle; suck throat lozenges.

HIGH ALTITUDE RAW THROAT

This is caused by breathing cold, dry air at high altitude.

Act: moisten the air by inhaling steam from a bowl, or sniff a billycan on the stove while brewing tea, but be careful not to scald your nose or throat. Expeditions never carry enough lozenges; if short, suck on hard candies. Drink plenty of fluid.

TONSILLITIS OR STREP THROAT

Yellow flecks of pus lie on the red swollen tonsils, glands under the angle of the jaw swell and swallowing hurts.

Rx: cephalosporin (D.2.1), salt-water gargles.

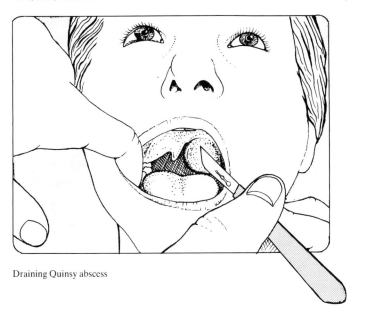

Draining Quinsy abscess

QUINSY
An abscess develops in the region of the tonsil bed, the soft palate swells and swallowing may became almost impossible.

Act: if medical help is far off, urgent decisive lancing with a sterile blade into the most swollen part of the affected tonsil releases a gush of pus, but this may be very difficult if the jaw is shut tight in spasm (trismus). Then gargle with warm salt-water.

Rx: cephalosporin (D.2.1).

GLANDULAR FEVER (Infectious mononucleosis)
The victim feels rotten, sluggish and washed-out for no apparent reason. A thick yellow slough in the sore throat looks far worse than it feels. Lymph glands in the neck, armpit and groin swell.

Act: rest is essential (ideally for four weeks) because the disease can recur with activity and, though rare, an enlarged spleen can rupture. It may take several months before the person feels full of vigour again.

If the throat swells so that swallowing and breathing are impaired, Rx: prednisone (D.4.1).

SWALLOWED FOREIGN BODY
Fish-bones stuck in the gullet may be dislodged and carried onwards by eating dry bread. An immovable chicken bone will have to be taken out by a surgeon. A piece of meat stuck in the gullet may threaten life; the Heimlich manoeuvre (see page 59) may dislodge it.

On rare occasions cricothyrotomy is needed.

Face and jaws

FRACTURE
The facial bones may be broken in several places in a bad smash. Suspect a fracture if the bite does not bring the teeth together normally, or if the victim has double vision, a bruised cheek, a black eye and you can feel a step in the line of his lower eye-socket bone.

Act: expert treatment is needed. Feed a fluid diet through a straw until the jaw can be fixed.

DISLOCATION
Rx: lorazepam (D.5.1) to relax the jaw. Support the lower jaw with the fingers of both hands, place your thumbs over his molars (padded to prevent him biting them), then push steadily down and backwards. The jaw should slide back into place.

HICCUP
Hiccup is a distressing and unpleasant rhythmic reflex contraction of the diaphragm and it needs to be interrupted.

Act: drink a cup of iced water fast; hold the breath or breathe into a paper bag; press on the eyeballs; or tickle the back of the throat with a feather – all to stimulate the vagus nerve.

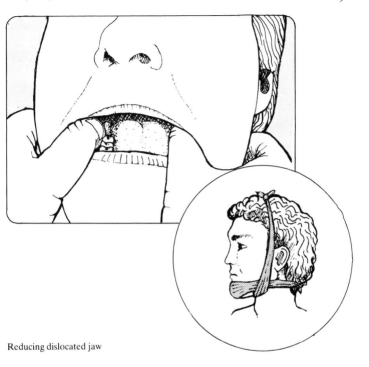

Reducing dislocated jaw

Teeth

Toothache can be so disabling as to render a climber useless, therefore it should be prevented by having a careful dental check before setting off on an expedition, eating a diet with adequate vitamin C, and cleaning the teeth regularly. In the absence of a toothbrush, rub the teeth with a wet finger covered with salt, or with a peeled green stick. Chewing gum cleans the mouth and exercises the gums.

Intense hot or cold makes diseased or exposed teeth painful, especially at high altitude. Cold teeth suddenly warmed by a hot drink, or biting on hard food may fracture. Dental pain comes under many disguises, aching, throbbing, searing, and it may be difficult to localize it to a particular tooth, especially in the early stages. Pain often affects adjacent teeth and may spread from the upper to the lower jaw and vice-versa, but never across the mid-line.

An amateur in the field can give only simple treatment in order to tide the victim over until he can see a proper dentist.

FINDING AN ACHING TOOTH

Tap the suspected tooth gently on the top and side with a metal instrument, preferably a blunt dental probe. A diseased tooth will hurt. Do not stick the point into the exposed cavity or into the softened exposed root. Cold and heat worsen pain in living teeth, although cold relieves discomfort in the early stage of a tooth abscess.

SINUSITIS

Pain from an infected maxillary sinus (the air space behind the prominence of the cheek) can mimic pain in the upper jaw; it is a common reason for faulty extraction of healthy teeth. In sinusitis pressing the cheek or knocking with a finger hurts; pain on both sides is unlikely to be dental. Pussy snot discharges from the nose.

COMMON CAUSES OF TOOTHACHE

Abscess – this forms round the root of a decaying tooth. The throbbing pain is partly relieved by clenching the jaw and then opening the mouth. The face and jaw swell, the breath stinks and pain is severe.

Act: hot salt mouth-washes are soothing, cleansing, and encourage pus to discharge into the mouth.

Rx: antibiotic (D.2.1), analgesic (D.1). Extract the tooth only as a last resort.

Cavity – a breach in the enamel due to decay, a lost filling or a fractured tooth which lays bare the sensitive inner dentine layer, or pulp of the tooth.

Act: use a temporary dressing of zinc oxide powder mixed with oil of cloves, or a synthetic tooth cement from a tube (which must be stoppered to prevent hardening). Do not dig out any filling remnants with a pointed dental probe. Push the dressing paste into the hole with a finger and press it down with a matchstick.

Exposed tooth root – when open to the cold exposed roots cause pain which, unattended, may develop into chronic toothache.
   Act: avoid heavy brushing and contact with heat or cold.

INFECTIONS
Bacterial (Vincent's infection, trench mouth) – poor oral hygiene allows plaque to grow next to the gums which become infected. The gums may swell painfully, bleed, and ulcerate causing an evil odour.
   Act: use a toothbrush carefully. Gentian violet paint made up from crystals, though messy to use, deals with most mouth ulcers.
   Rx: antibiotics (D.2).

Pericoronitis – food debris collects under the gingival flap over a partially-erupted third molar tooth. Infection starts, the gums swell and are further traumatized when pinched in chewing. Soon the person is unable to chew and the mouth is foul and painful.
   Act: vigorous rinsing with hot salt-water. If possible use a bent hypodermic needle to reach under the flap into the crevices of the gum and flush out pus and debris with salt-water.
   Rx: antibiotics (D.2).

DISLOCATED OR AVULSED TEETH
Use warm salt mouthwash, replace the tooth immediately in the socket, and try to stabilize it. It may 'take' like a free graft.

TOOTH EXTRACTION
If far from help it may be best to extract a very painful tooth and allow someone, who would otherwise be an invalid, to continue with the expedition. If closer to help take out a tooth only as a last resort, because skilful dentists can renovate some awful looking teeth. The art of extracting a loose or a bad tooth can be learned

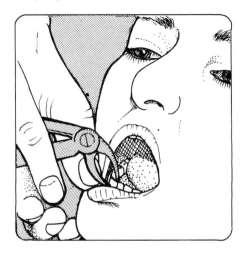

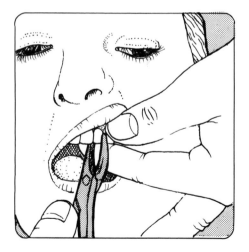

Lower and upper dental forceps

easily enough, but to remove a strong, live tooth is very difficult. You need the proper tools, preferably some local anaesthetic, and a stoical patient. Lessons on how to inject local anaesthetic should be taken from a dental surgeon before leaving on an expedition.

Rx: antibiotic (D.2) before attempting extraction; local anaesthetic, lignocaine 2 per cent (D.17.1) with adrenaline 2 ml for each tooth. This may not be effective if swelling is severe.

Upper jaw – insert the needle just through the skin where the gum and the cheek join, near the apex of the affected tooth. Put in a few drops to start freezing; after two minutes advance the needle and distribute the remainder of the 2 ml around the tooth. Do the same on the palate side where there will be more resistance because the tissues are tight.

Lower jaw – local anaesthetic placed as described above may be effective from the premolars forward. Behind the molars a mandibular block is needed and this requires skill.

When the tooth is anaesthetized, or the patient is sufficiently drugged to allow the ordeal, grasp the tooth with a pair of upper or lower dental forceps. Push the beaks of the forceps down each side of the tooth below the gum margin, in order to get a hold as far down the root as possible. Use a sideways rocking and rotating movement to work the tooth loose. A disturbing crunching comes from the jaw as the roots separate from the socket. If the tooth breaks try to remove the remaining fragments but do not dig deeply for them or the socket may bleed profusely. Pinch the gums together to stop bleeding and have the victim bite on a damp gauze pack or paper tissue for fifteen minutes. If it still does not stop, pack the socket with gauze. Even removing the tooth crown alone may diminish the pain by letting pus discharge down the roots into the mouth. Smoking may restart the bleeding so desist for a day. Start hot salt mouth-washes on the second day.

17 Hypothermia

Hypothermia is generalized cold-injury. Local freezing cold-injury is frost-bite; without freezing it is immersion-injury. Both hypothermia and frost-bite may co-exist, but hypothermia takes precedence in treatment because it may be fatal.

Hypothermia describes the consequence of body-chilling, which is worsened by wet-cold, exhaustion, anxiety and injury. Wet and wind are a lethal combination and chill a person more than dry-cold, so hypothermia occurs on Dartmoor or Ben Nevis more readily than in the Yukon.

Denizens of polar climates and high altitudes, aware of the dangers of cold, dress in warm protective clothing. Inuit, Tibetans, Andean Indians and barefoot Himalayan hillmen survive intuitively in their hostile environment and appear to adapt to cold. But, if careless, all these people can suffer the ravages of cold like the rest of us unless they practise common-sense prevention.

Prevention

Plan even the shortest outdoor expedition carefully, watch for early signs of hypothermia and act promptly to avert it. Gauge the day's activity to the party's weakest member. Distance and speed of travel vary with terrain, weather and load. Walking too far too fast, carrying too heavy a load and being cold, exhausted, hungry and demoralized, are the corner-stones of exposure. If the weather changes, be prepared to abandon the original plan and take an easier, shorter route home. The measure of a good outdoorsman is knowing when to turn around.

Children and adolescents withstand cold less well than adults because their surface area is larger in proportion to their weight, and they generally carry less subcutaneous fat. With less experience and smaller reserves of stamina and mental fibre, they tend to flag and give up hope unless strongly led. Women, by reason of their subcutaneous fat, are better insulated than men.

Temperature control

The temperature of the central core of the body, which houses the vital organs (brain, heart, lungs and kidneys), is preserved at the expense of the surrounding shell (muscles, subcutaneous fat and skin). A temperature-regulating centre in the brain senses changes in the temperature of blood flowing through it and maintains a balance between heat-gain and heat-loss. Hypothermia occurs when more heat is lost than is produced.

A rise or fall in core temperature of 2°C causes noticeable symptoms; a drop of more than 5°C can kill. Core temperature is measured with a special low-reading thermometer, below 35° C (95°F), placed in the rectum, an awkward manoeuvre in someone fully dressed. Mouth and armpit temperatures are often several degrees below the rectal temperature, depending on environmental conditions.

CONSERVATION OF BODY HEAT

Insulation – air and fat are poor conductors and therefore good insulators. Animals, when cold, raise their fur in order to trap air; likewise humans get goose-bumps. Wool, polypropylene and pile partially insulate by trapping air in the interstices of their cellular structure, which does not collapse when wet as does goose- or eider-down. The more layers of clothing, the better the insulation. Water is an excellent conductor and thus destroys insulation. The early climbers of Everest went to over 28,000 ft dressed in Norfolk-tweed jackets, breeches dipped in water-repelling alum, several layers of Shetland-wool pullovers, and long wool stockings.

Wind-proof, water-proof fabrics prevent entrapped insulating air being displaced and also diminish convection, conduction and evaporation. Breathable fabrics like Gortex allow some ventilation; coated nylon does not, so water condenses on the inside of an outer garment and soaks the clothing underneath. Cotton jeans offer poor protection from the cold and wet. Sitting on a mattress or rucksack provides insulation from the cold ground.

Heat gain and loss

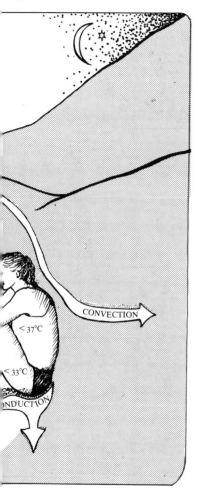

Blood-vessel constriction – in the cold, an automatic reflex control causes the smooth muscles in the blood-vessels of the shell to constrict and thus keep warm blood circulating in the core preventing heat-loss from the shell.

LOSS OF BODY HEAT

Convection – wind-speed determines the chill felt at an even temperature; air temperature alone is meaningless as a physiological measure of cold. On a windless, sunny day at −40°C (-40°F) you can walk about lightly clad owing to solar radiation, but the least puff of wind will send you scurrying for shelter. At 0°C (32°F) with a 65 kph (40 mph) wind, cold may be intolerable. Wet-cold feels much chillier than dry-cold because conduction and evaporation are increased. The wind-chill index is a graphic plot of wind-speed against temperature. Wind destroys air insulation by displacing trapped air, energy is expended in battling the wind and evaporation increased by wind blowing on a wet surface.

Convection also continues in the absence of wind because air next to the skin is warmed and rises away from the body. Heat is lost quickly from an uncovered head; so when your feet are cold put on a hat. Wear a wool scarf, make a snug fit at the wrists with Velcro or elastic and tuck trousers into socks or use gaiters. Mittens allow fingers to warm each other by mutual contact, whereas gloves isolate each digit. Silk gloves allow delicate touch, for example when handling a camera, and can be worn inside mittens.

Conduction – heat flows by conduction directly from a warm body to wet clothes and to the cold ground. Wind and wet reduce insulation of clothing to one tenth of normal. During glacial stream crossings always wear long trousers for warmth, boots for sure-footing and belay securely with a rope. Legs immersed to the thigh cool quickly; they move slower and slower, and may finally collapse leading to drowning.

Evaporation – to evaporate 1 g of water requires 540 calories of heat. Body evaporation is caused by:

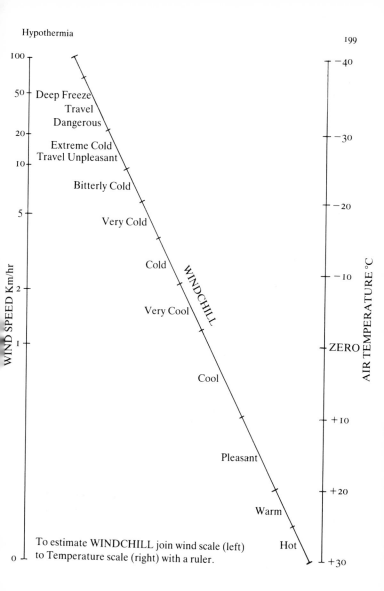

WIND SPEED Km/hr

AIR TEMPERATURE °C

Deep Freeze
Travel
Dangerous

Extreme Cold
Travel Unpleasant

Bitterly Cold

Very Cold

Cold

WINDCHILL

Very Cool

Cool

Pleasant

Warm

Hot

ZERO

To estimate WINDCHILL join wind scale (left)
to Temperature scale (right) with a ruler.

Sweating: 0.5 litre (1 pint) of fluid is normally lost daily through the skin, much more in hot climates and in dry-cold. During heavy exercise up to 1 litre may be lost each hour.

Breathing: warm breath condenses in cold air, and breathing cold air cools the airway. Much water can be lost during heavy breathing.

Blood-vessel dilation – alcohol dilates blood-vessels causing warm blood to flow away from the core to the periphery. Drunks found dead in snow banks sometimes have thrown off their clothes because a flush of warm blood suffuses the body after the sympathetic nervous system finally breaks down. A nip of brandy may do wonders for the spirit of a cold, demoralized person, but too much alcohol makes the body less aware of cold, hence St Bernard dogs are now ostracized. Alcohol can cause a sudden fall in blood-sugar (hypoglycaemia), especially when taken before exercise, because it depresses the mobilization of glucose from muscle glycogen stores. So always hand out candies before passing round the hip-flask.

INCREASE IN BODY HEAT

Radiation – sun and fire heat directly by radiation.

Exercise – voluntary muscle work can produce up to fifteen times the normal amount of body heat; involuntary shivering six times. Exhaustion, or inadequate food or water, precludes shivering and exercise.

Food – metabolism of food produces energy which is converted into heat. Heavy work requires 4,000 calories each day, equivalent to the energy consumed by walking round the Snowdon Horseshoe, 20 rkm (12 miles) and climbing 750 m (2,500 ft). Carbohydrate is most quickly absorbed as sugar. Hot food and drink boost morale, but transfer little heat to the stomach. Beware of eating snow to slake thirst; the same amount of heat is needed to melt snow to water as to bring that water to the boil.

Symptoms and signs

MILD HYPOTHERMIA

Core temperature 37° C–33° C (98° F–91° F). The victim can usually still talk; he grumbles, and mumbles about feeling cold, stiff muscles, and cramps. Skin is cold, pale and blue-grey owing to constricted blood-vessels and sluggish circulation. Uncharacteristic behaviour is common but may be obvious only to someone who knows his usual personality and performance. Excitement, lethargy, poor judgement and decision-making are common features. Therefore he must never be left alone on the mountain, or allowed to descend alone.

At a core temperature of about 35° C (95° F), he fumbles and stumbles because of poor muscular co-ordination. The brain is fuddled and he may hallucinate and shiver uncontrollably.

Act: the leader must decide whether to get down off the mountain away from the cold, wind and wet, or to stay put, shelter and summon help, which may take several hours to arrive.

If the victim appears fit to go on, rest first. Shelter out of the wind, eat some food and brew a hot drink. Thus boosted he may be able to descend unaided. But do not sit around too long or he may cool further, as will his companions. Descend at his pace, not yours, to a camp or hut where he can be thoroughly warmed.

SEVERE HYPOTHERMIA

Core temperature below 32° C (90° F). Severe hypothermia is common in mountains, especially in wet and cold; it also occurs in urban life to alcoholics and very old people.

Shivering stops and with it disappears the victim's last self-protective mechanism. His behaviour may be irrational and apathetic, or aggressive and violent. Muscles become rigid and movement is un-coordinated, breathing quickens and pupils are dilated. He may have a seizure and slip into a coma. An irregular pulse heralds loss of control of the heart-beat. This all happens fast, and kills. The body-core needs heat urgently during the first half-hour after rescue.

Act: On the mountain:

Shelter – stop and shelter the victim out of wind, rain and snow.
Erect a tent, dig a snow hole, build a lean-to, or put him in a
bivouac sack or a strong polythene bag. Insulate him well from the
cold ground with a closed-cell foam mattress, rucksacks or foliage
and grass. A fit team-member should climb naked into a
sleeping-bag beside the unclothed victim; let's hope they're friends.
Inside the sleeping-bag place a hot water-bottle, or heated stones
wrapped in cloth to prevent burning, or use commercially produced
heat-packs. Allow the victim to fall asleep if he is fully re-warmed.
When he is warm dress him in dry clothes. Some experts claim that
sleeping-bag re-warming is even better than a hot bath because the
risk of heart irregularities is less.

Rescue – other members of the party may also be cold and miserable
and will need sustenance for the long, hard job of rescue. Crowd
into a shelter, light a stove and brew a drink – even a single candle
will warm a small enclosed space. But beware of poisonous carbon
monoxide gas accumulating from stoves.

Leave at least one person to look after the victim. Send the
strongest competent member of the party for help, having agreed
on a signal to direct arriving rescuers to the victim. Calculate the
map reference and send it together with a written message about the
condition of the victim. Radios and helicopters have greatly
simplified modern rescues.

Having decided to stay put and shelter, do not waver even if the
victim improves; by starting down he may relapse, and you may
miss the rescuers. Making a hypothermic person walk will further
exhaust him. However, if forced to carry him immobile on a
stretcher, remember he may continue to cool, so wrap him well.

If you have to descend because help is unavailable, plan an
escape route that avoids ridges and windy places. If the victim is on
a stretcher handle him very gently to avoid triggering lethal heart
irregularities (arrythmias) and carry him head slightly downhill to
maintain his blood-pressure. One person should watch him closely
all the time. Ideally, start intravenous fluids on the mountain before
the evacuation begins.

Inhaling warm humidified air – re-warming can be started on the mountain with a portable apparatus which provides heat that is transferred directly to the core via the big blood-vessels of the neck and chest; it also prevents further heat-loss from expired air. But such first-aid treatment in the field is only an adjunct to adequate body insulation.

In one system (U-Vic Heat Treat) air, or oxygen, passes through a heater-vaporizer unit at 70° C and into a reservoir re-breathing bag attached to a mask. Another system (Lloyd) generates heat and moisture by passing oxygen through soda-lime previously charged with a pre-set volume of carbon dioxide. The temperature and humidity depend on the volume of carbon dioxide added.

At Base Camp:

Hot bath re-warming – provided the victim is conscious, but not colder than 32° C (90° F), re-warm him in a bath of water kept at about 42° C (111° F). Water at this temperature feels comfortable to the hand. Put him in the bath fully clothed; removing clothes may be difficult because hypothermics curl into the foetal position. When warm, remove his clothes, cutting them off if necessary. Cold, wet clothes and a cold body cool the bath-water, so top it up frequently with hot water, stirring continuously.

Submerge the victim in the warm water. Make sure his limbs are immersed, otherwise blood will pool in the periphery depriving the central core of precious oxygen needed to nourish the brain and heart.

Keep the victim in the bath until both core and extremities are thoroughly re-warmed; a tide of cold blood returning from the limbs will cool the core again (after-drop). The blood will carry acid breakdown products of metabolism, especially potassium, which cause dangerous heart arrythmias. Be especially vigilant for arrythmias when re-warming anyone who is unconscious, under ten or over seventy years of age, or who has a history of heart disease. Saunas are great after skiing, but are of little use re-warming hypothermia victims because the intense heat causes sudden massive dilatation of peripheral blood-vessels with little alteration in core temperature.

If the victim starts violent shivering during the re-warming process, control the pain with strong analgesic drugs. When the rectal temperature reaches about 36° C (97° F) remove him from the bath and place him, tilted slightly head down, in a warm bed in a warm room. During the next hour he may collapse from re-warming shock; blood-pressure falls and the pulse rises above 160 beats per minute and may be irregular. Arrythmias are difficult to diagnose in the field; all are bad news. A vigorous thump at the base of the breast-bone (sternum) may, with luck, restore auricular fibrillation to normal; with ventricular irregularities prayer alone must suffice until he reaches hospital.

Fluid replacement – all hypothermic victims are short of fluid (dehydration). Re-warming in a hot bath inevitably shunts blood from core to shell, causing more dehydration and shock. So give lots of fluid by mouth, provided he is conscious.

If intravenous fluid is available give 1–2 litres of Ringer's lactate or normal saline immediately. Follow this with five per cent dextrose-water (500 ml six-hourly), in order to help transfer glucose across cell membranes and to move potassium back into the cells. Place the i/v bag under his bum so his body weight makes a head of pressure, warms the fluid and prevents it freezing. Give sodium bicarbonate (50 mEq in 50 ml = 1 ampoule) in the first bag of fluid in order to neutralize the acidity of the blood.

Other re-warming methods are possible only in a well-equipped hospital.

Peritoneal dialysis: flushing warm dialysate fluid round the abdominal peritoneal cavity provides heat directly to the core, and helps the body fluid equilibrate with the dialysate.

Extra-corporeal re-warming via cardio-pulmonary by-pass: provides total control and is ideal for the desperately-ill, severely-hypothermic patient.

IMMERSION HYPOTHERMIA
Immersion hypothermia differs from mountain exposure in its rapid onset, lack of shivering and faster cooling when exercising. Water causes rapid heat-loss because of the great speed at which it conducts heat away from the body and the large amount of heat

needed to raise its temperature. The victim may drown because hypothermia causes loss of consciousness.

Experiments on volunteers have shown that subjects lightly clothed, floating motionless and immersed to the neck will reach 'incipient death' in two and a half to three hours at 10° C (50° F), in two hours at 5° C (41° F), and in one and a half hours at 0° C (32° F).

A person can swim less that 1 km in water at 10° C (50° F), so it will usually be safer to stay with an upturned boat than to strike out for shore. Lying huddled in a crouch minimizes heat-loss from thermogenic areas of the axilla and groin, and prevents the victim burning calories in fruitless attempts to swim 'to keep warm'. A personal flotation device prolongs survival by three times. Wool insulates better than any other normal clothing when wet. Covering the head reduces heat-loss from convection by half. It is warmer out of the water clinging to an upturned boat, despite wind and rain, than staying immersed. Staying with the boat also increases the chance of being spotted by searchers. Despair is the overwhelming emotion of a shipwreck victim, who is inclined not to bother with such details of survival skills which can tip the balance from death to life.

DEEP HYPOTHERMIA

At core temperatures below 28° C (82° F) life becomes suspended, like an animal in hibernation, and the victim of such severe hypothermia may appear dead. He does not shiver, muscles are stiff as in rigor mortis and skin is pale and bloodless. Heartbeat and breathing are barely perceptible. But although oxygen for the brain and heart is greatly diminished, it may be adequate for their needs at that temperature.

Declare a victim of hypothermia dead only if he is warm and dead; that is, he has failed to revive after adequate re-warming. A severely hypothermic victim who is still alive may have fixed and dilated pupils, a common sign of death. Do not give up easily; 'corpses' have been known to wake up in a warm mortuary. The only sure signs are a lack of response when the victim is re-warmed, and ECG evidence of the heart having stopped.

18 Frost-bite

Frost-bite is localized freezing of tissue of the body shell affecting the face, hands and feet most commonly. Hypothermia, by contrast, is generalized cooling of the deep inner core, and contributes to frost-bite. If the core remains warm the extremities are less likely to freeze in severe cold weather.

After an accident damaged tissue freezes readily and the chance of frost-bite increases because the victim may be immobilized by pain and therefore unable to exercise to produce heat. Likewise, shivering may be abolished if the victim is unconscious. Blood-loss from an open wound, or into a closed fracture, causes clinical shock; vessels in the extremities constrict shunting blood from the limbs to the core in order to maintain vital functions. Emotional shock caused by fear resulting from an accident has similar results.

At high altitude the risk of frost-bite is great because less oxygen is available to nourish the tissues. Over 6,000 m (20,000 ft) work is exhausting, sleep is elusive, and the brain is dulled, so common-sense precautions against cold are forgotten. When Herzog dropped his gloves on Annapurna in 1950, he forgot about the spare pair of socks in his rucksack which, used as mittens, could have saved his fingers. Cold deserves profound respect; frost-bite is generally avoidable but it can catch the unwary causing devastating disability.

Prevention

BODY PROTECTION
A wind-proof, water-proof suit protects against hypothermia. When insulation is destroyed by wind and water the body core cools and the extremities are in danger of frost-bite.

FEET
Tight boots cramp the circulation and cause blisters. Broken skin is liable to cold-injury and infection. Stop and remove boots as soon as the feet feel very cold or begin to lose sensation. Early warming

may prevent trouble later. Wear gaiters to keep out snow. Carry spare dry socks, which can double as mittens; a wrinkled sock in a boot causes uneven pressure and interferes with blood-flow. Wind-proof trousers keep the legs warm, and hence the feet.

A plastic bag pulled over the foot next to the skin makes a vapour-barrier liner which traps the warm moisture of sweating feet preventing socks from becoming soaked. At $-40°$ C ($-40°$ F) and zero humidity the feet are quite comfortable and, surprisingly, do not feel as if they are standing in a swamp. Rubber vapour-barrier boots are very warm but bulky; good for plodding round camp, but clumsy for technical climbing. Modern plastic double-skinned climbing boots are warm, waterproof and do not freeze unlike their leather equivalents.

HANDS

Outer mittens allow fingers to move freely and to warm each other by contact, whereas gloves isolate each finger. Clothed hands still need to be able to handle rope, ice-axe and crampon straps. In severe cold, get in the habit of doing all routine tasks wearing mittens because each time they are removed hands cool quickly. Silk or polypropylene gloves can be worn if mittens have to be removed for performing delicate tasks such as handling cold metal, for example a camera. Elastic cuffs of anoraks and mittens should not be tight. In extreme cold, skin sticks to freezing metal so beware of metal spoons and mugs, and never hold metal between the lips.

FACE

The face is difficult to cover completely even with Dracula-like neoprene face-masks; ears and noses cool fast because a large area of skin projects from the face. A signal mirror carried in the pocket allows frequent inspection of cheeks and nose for white patches of frost-nip, which appear before any pain is felt. A balaclava wool hat leaves a visor opening and protects most of the face. A scarf tied loosely over the mouth and nose soon ices up with frozen breath forming a barrier to the cold air. Breathing very cold air can cause wheeze like asthma and if prolonged can damage the small terminal air sacs of the lung (sometimes referred to as frozen lung).

GENITALS

Men have the bigger problem. Fortified under-pants, a rabbit skin or newspaper stuffed down the front will keep everything warm. Dipping in brandy does not help.

Once frost-bitten, a person seems more susceptible to frost-bite again in the same place, owing to local nerve damage.

MECHANISM OF FROST-BITE

Fluid within the cell freezes, the nucleus bursts and the cell dies. Breakdown products of frozen cells are released on re-warming and further damage the tissues. Small arteries in the shell constrict in response to messages from the temperature-regulating centre in the brain. So warm blood flows to the core at the expense of the extremities, which freeze. Capillaries are damaged by freezing and leak, causing blisters. Cold red blood cells sludge and clot in the small vessels, preventing oxygen reaching the tissues.

Climbers at high altitude often have to weather out storms in their tents; they are unable to exercise enough to stimulate circulation, and fail to drink enough because fuel for melting snow is scarce. Red blood cells multiply in response to oxygen lack, causing the blood to become viscous and to flow sluggishly. Small clots form in the leg veins, pieces break off and lodge in the limbs and the lungs.

Symptoms and signs

Frost-bite behaves like a skin burn and may be superficial or deep, depending on whether there is damage to the germinal layer of the skin from which new cells arise. Depth of freezing depends on temperature and length of exposure to cold.

SUPERFICIAL FROST-BITE

Superficial freezing (frost-nip) damages only the surface cells, so complete healing can be expected without loss of tissue. Frozen tissue is white, waxy and feels intensely cold, but it is soft and resilient when pressed. The skin tingles and is painful, indicating undamaged nerves. Blisters may form.

Act: jump up and down to get warm, wriggle toes, flex ankles, clap hands and swing arms. Put a cold hand in your own armpit or crotch, or pee on your fingers. Place a cold foot against the warm trunk of a fit, sympathetic companion. If ears or nose feel numb hold a warm hand against them, or ask a friend to breathe on them. Rubbing the skin vigorously may break the surface and allow infection to enter. Never rub snow into a frozen part because snow crystals act like broken glass. Numbness wears off as the part thaws giving way to excruciating burning pain.

Rx: strong analgesics (D.1.3 or 4).

DEEP FROST-BITE

Deep freezing kills tissue and nerves with insidious loss of pain and cold sensation. Skin forms blisters and turns a mottled blue. Frozen tissue feels solid to touch; muscle may be frozen, but tendon is usually spared and frost-bitten limbs can still move. The ugly appearance of frost-bite, ranging from a patch of black skin, to gangrene of the whole limb, is a poor guide to how much tissue will die eventually – so do not be hasty with the knife.

Act: In the field: rest the frozen limb and keep it clean to prevent infection, dead slough will usually separate from healthy tissue in two to three months provided there is no infection or further damage. Cells at the edge of an area of frost-bite are balanced precariously between life and death and need molly-coddling in order to ensure they survive. Do not risk infection by pricking blisters, which if left alone, dry over several weeks forming a black crusted scab. Cover the wound with a plain, dry, non-stick dressing. Splint the limb.

A deeply frozen limb feels tight, and is difficult to move; later it swells. Elevate the limb on a rucksack above body level to enable oedema fluid to drain away. Once a limb is thawed keep it warm, at rest and protected from further injury.

A re-warmed and thawed climber should preferably be carried off the mountain on a stretcher. It is better to walk off the mountain with feet still frozen, before allowing them to re-warm because thawing and re-freezing does more damage than walking on frozen feet. Drain blisters with a sterile needle because they will break anyway while walking; then dress them cleanly. In remote regions the victim will have to rest at night and re-warming is inevitable. Just do the best you can.

In the valley: a frost-bitten climber may also be suffering from exposure. When he reaches a shelter or base camp warm him thoroughly and make him comfortable. Give plenty of fluids. A wee dram of spirits will cheer, but forbid smoking because nicotine can halve the calibre of small arteries. Treat pain and anxiety; then thaw the limb.

Thawing – rapid thawing is less damaging to frost-bitten tissue than slow re-warming; the limb is frozen for a shorter time and subsequent swelling subsides more quickly. Ice formed between cells melts, and salts move across the walls upsetting cell chemistry. Stagnant blood starts to recirculate carrying away poisonous chemicals formed during thawing.

Rapid thawing can only be done at a base camp where adequate fuel and large containers of water are available. Never thaw a limb in front of an open flame as the flesh may cook. Immerse the frozen limb for twenty to forty minutes in water at about 42° C (105° F); this feels pleasantly warm to the uninjured hand, but using a thermometer is preferable. At any greater heat the water will boil tissue. The frozen limb cools the water-bath so stir in more warm water frequently. Do not heat the bath directly as the temperature cannot then be controlled. Continue thawing until the warmed tissue is soft, pliable and flushed red. Pain may be severe (see below).

Cleaning and dressing – after washing your own hands thoroughly with soap and boiled water, clean the frost-bitten area daily with a saline solution made with a tablespoon of salt in a litre of boiled water. Gentle dabbing is sufficient; do not scrub the skin surface. Dry fingers or toes and separate them with dry cotton wool.

If possible leave the frozen part open to the air to allow a scab to form. But do not be tempted to pick at the black scab, which protects underlying healing tissue and must be nurtured like a seed bed.

Take scrupulous care to avoid infection which will convert a dry
healing scab into soggy, inflamed, wet gangrene that spreads up the
limb destroying as it goes. If the wound has to be dressed, use a
sulpha cream and change the dressing at least daily. Exercise the
part continually to prevent contracture of joints.

Drugs – antibiotics: give a broad-spectrum antibiotic,
co-trimoxazole (D.2.2) especially if the line between healthy and
dead tissue becomes inflamed. Double the dose if it looks red and
inflamed, feels tender and throbs.
– Pain relief: Rx: morphine (D.1.4), or codeine (D.1.3).
– Tetanus toxoid: get a booster dose as soon as possible.

Medical sympathectomy: [phenoxybenzamine] 10 mg twice daily for six
days may counter vaso-constriction.
Vaso-dilators (Ronicol, Priscol): these drugs used to be fashionable
among climbers but have no place in the field treatment of frost-bite.
They cause vessels to dilate, giving a deceptively pleasant feeling of
warmth as blood surges to the skin surface; but they do nothing for the
frost-bitten part and much heat is lost with further danger of
hypothermia.

HOSPITAL
Sympathectomy (surgical): may help if done in the first twenty-four to
forty-eight hours after freezing.
Fasciotomy: should be done early to relieve oedema causing pressure on
small vessels to the hands or in muscle compartments.
Amputation: may be needed eventually, but it should be delayed until
natural separation has taken place. Frost-bite in January means
amputation in July.

Eschew heroic surgery in the field; spreading gangrene is the only
indication for emergency amputation. Guess generously at the
extent of irreparable damage; notoriously evil-looking limbs can,
and do, recover almost completely.

Other types of cold injury

IMMERSION (TRENCH) FOOT
A non-freezing cold injury caused by prolonged exposure to cold and wet. Mild numbness and a feeling of never being warm may progress to a freezing cold-injury (frost-bite).

CHILBLAINS
Repeated exposure of bare skin to wet, wind and cold causes red, itchy, tender, swollen skin.

19 Acclimatization

Acclimatization starts at about 1,500 m (c 5,000 ft) and allows humans to live and work in the oxygen-thin atmosphere of high altitude (above 2,500 m, c 8,000 ft). The air breathed at sea-level has four parts nitrogen, and one part oxygen. As we climb the 4:1 ratio of these gases does not change, but their density becomes less; fewer molecules are bouncing around in a given volume of air and the pressure exerted by them falls steadily. Thus an ordinary weather barometer can be used as an altimeter because it registers the pressure gases exert on the earth's surface. At the top of Mt Everest (8,848 m, 29,028 ft) the atmospheric pressure is less than one third that at sea-level. Eventually the pressure is no longer adequate to drive sufficient nourishing oxygen into the tissues, especially the nerve cells which demand the most; brain cells deprived of oxygen die in less than four minutes.

Life would be unendurable above 3,000 m (c 10,000 ft) without the physiological adjustments of acclimatization, which compensate for the low pressure of oxygen in the air, and high altitude mountaineering would be impossible. Certainly no man could climb to the top of Mt Everest without oxygen, a feat now achieved several times.

THE INITIAL RAPID PHASE OF ACCLIMATIZATION (from 1,500 m, c 5,000 ft)
Breathing: at sea-level the rate and depth of breathing are controlled by the level of carbon dioxide waste produced by body tissues burning oxygen. Above 3,000 m (c 10,000 ft) carbon dioxide control is over-ridden by the paramount need to get enough oxygen. Low oxygen pressure in the atmosphere, and hence in the lungs and blood (hypoxia) increases the rate and depth of breathing, so carbon dioxide levels in the blood fall briskly until a steady state is reached for that individual at that altitude.

Breathing rate increases because hypoxia triggers the carotid chemo-receptor organs in the neck to stimulate the respiratory centre in the brain. With deeper breathing, carbon dioxide, which dilutes oxygen in the lungs, is removed more rapidly; its concentration in the blood falls, which in turn dampens the activity of the respiratory centre. A delicate balance is struck between two opposing forces, low oxygen and low carbon dioxide pressure, which control the rate and depth of breathing.

Increased ventilation of the lungs, especially on exercise, provides more oxygen for absorption by the capillaries. On the other hand, at altitude the accessory breathing muscles (diaphragm, abdomen, intercostals and neck) burn oxygen, so less is available for the hard work of climbing. Low carbon dioxide makes the blood more alkaline and so to compensate, more bicarbonate is excreted by the kidneys.

Breathing rhythm commonly changes at altitude, particularly at night; it steadily deepens, rises to a crescendo, then falls off and finally, ceases completely for several seconds. Then the pattern starts over again. Carbon dioxide in the blood builds to a level where it stimulates the respiratory centre. Breathing then restarts, carbon dioxide is blown off, the stimulus lessens, and breathing comes to a standstill. With acclimatization this abnormal behaviour of the respiratory centre, known as *Cheyne Stokes periodic breathing*, settles down to a new level of stimulation by carbon dioxide.

Heart: the heart beats faster and more strongly, thus increasing the flow of blood (cardiac output). The climber will feel thumping palpitations in the chest and a dull headache throbbing in time with the pulse.

Hypoxia stimulates both the carotid chemo-receptors and the sympathetic nervous system making the heart pump more blood to the lungs. Thereby more oxygen is available to the tissues where it is readily released because of the relative difference in pressure between blood and tissue cells. Many capillaries open to carry more blood to the cells. Pressure in the pulmonary artery rises so lung capillaries are better perfused and the surface area for gas exchange is increased.

THE LATER, SLOWER PHASE OF ACCLIMATIZATION

Blood and plasma: soon after arriving at altitude the volume of plasma, the fluid in which blood cells are suspended, falls by twenty to thirty per cent. This is partly because more urine is passed at altitude, partly because of dehydration caused by sweating with heavy exercise and overbreathing in the cold dry atmosphere, and partly because of a proven shift from the extracellular to the intracellular space. Water losses are hard to replenish above the snow-line because fuel is scarce for melting snow to provide the normal daily requirement of 4–5 litres of water and stoves work less efficiently at altitude.

Hypoxia immediately stimulates bone marrow to produce more red cells in proportion to the severity of oxygen deficiency. As a result more haemoglobin is produced to carry more oxygen. At high altitude blood can carry up to half as much oxygen again as at sea-level. As red cells increase and plasma diminishes, blood becomes more viscous putting a greater strain on the heart. The circulation becomes sluggish reducing oxygen delivery to the tissues. Red cells clump forming clots, and stack together lessening the surface area for oxygen diffusion. The lazy calf muscles of storm-bound climbers fail to compress the leg veins which should normally pump blood efficiently back to the heart.

Tissues: blood is shunted from non-essential to vital tissues (brain, heart and lungs). Adaptations in the cells assist the release and uptake of oxygen by mitochondria, the power units of cells. Several complex physiological changes lead towards more efficient use of oxygen; new capillary formation, increased muscle myoglobin and cytochrome oxidase.

Acclimatization changes have one common purpose: to make optimum use of what little oxygen is available in the thin air on high. But ironically some of these adaptations defeat their own ends, for example the blunted response of Sherpas to hypoxia.

Acclimatization is quite idiosyncratic; it starts at different altitudes and proceeds at different rates in different people. Some people are never troubled provided they ascend slowly enough, while others, for no obvious physical reason, never acclimatize properly however long they remain high even at a relatively low altitude.

Acclimatization is not progressive. After about three months at very high altitude, say above 6,000 m (c 20,000 ft), the climber steadily deteriorates. He sleeps and works poorly, and loses appetite and weight. A retreat to the valleys for a long holiday is the solution.

20   Acute Mountain Sickness

Acute Mountain Sickness (AMS) is caused by diminished oxygen pressure in the atmosphere, and hence in the blood (hypoxia), and strikes those failing to adapt to high altitude, above 2,500 m. Anyone venturing into the high, cold, thin air is wise to study AMS, which can kill the unwary, the bold and the previously healthy. It affects those who ascend too high too fast, and is usually cured by immediate descent. AMS is sometimes fatal, but it need not be.

Mild AMS has vague, ill-defined symptoms; headache, insomnia, fatigue, poor appetite, nausea, dizziness and breathlessness, and can drift subtly into the more dangerous severe AMS, which can kill. Hypoxia sets off a chain of events, but it is only part of the story. The real problem is body-water settling in the wrong places; the brain in High Altitude Cerebral Oedema (HACO); and/or the lungs in High Altitude Pulmonary Oedema (HAPO); and/or the tissues of the face, hands and feet.

Mild AMS

Many people who climb high (over 2,500 m, c 8,000 ft) are fit on arrival, but feel ghastly over the next couple of days with headache, fatigue, poor appetite and breathlessness. These symptoms usually pass off as they adapt to the low pressure of oxygen in the air. Some climbers never get used to the altitude, their symptoms become worse and worse and some die from HACO or HAPO.

PREDICTING AMS

No one can predict who will suffer from AMS, whether it will be mild or severe or when it will strike. Climbers who have performed well at altitude will probably do so again each time they go high. Those who have suffered AMS before may suffer again, and at a similar altitude. Fitness and training guarantee no protection, the sexes succumb equally, and no age is exempt. The young appear more prone, regardless of exercise and rate of ascent. Weight gain during the ascent means water retention which bodes ill.

PREVENTING AMS

Allow ample time at various levels to acclimatize. AMS is likely to occur the higher, the faster, the harder and the longer the climb. Cold and wind, fear and fatigue, dehydration during rapid ascent, and strenuous exercise soon after, and upper respiratory infection all predispose the climber to AMS.

Climb without haste – above 4,000 m (c 13,000 ft) gain height slowly and steadily at about 300 m a day with a rest day every 1,000 m. Avoid strenuous exertion soon after arriving at altitude. On expeditions, carry loads high, dump them and descend in order to sleep low. Keep loads light and rest frequently. High mountains should be approached at a leisurely pace both for pleasure and safety. The first Everest climbers always did so during their march through Tibet. They achieved Herculean feats, reaching over 8,500 m (28,000 ft) in the early 1920s with primitive equipment and clothing, and oxygen apparatus which they rarely used because it was so heavy and clumsy.

Drink sufficient fluid – 4–5 litres, about 16–20 cups daily, should balance the heavy fluid loss caused by strenuous breathing in dry, cold, thin air and maintain clear, colourless and plentiful urine; 1 litre daily, about two bursting bladder-fulls, is the mimimum acceptable. Dark-yellow urine is concentrated, usually indicating dehydration; it may however be part of the water retention of AMS. Avoid alcohol, a hangover simulates AMS and may confuse the diagnosis.

Eat a high calorie diet – with plenty of carbohydrate before and during ascent. A good appetite suggests good acclimatization. Don't take salt or sedatives.

If, despite these precautions, a climber gets sick and does not improve on rest, **descend** quickly until he starts to feel better. Even 300 m will help; 1,000 m may be magical.

Beware the climber who acclimatizes poorly coping less well than expected for the altitude and his previous performance. Macho types who battle ever upward despite worsening distress are those likely to end up buried under a cairn of stones on the glacier.

SYMPTOMS AND SIGNS
These develop twelve to forty-eight hours after arriving at altitude.

Headache – the head feels tight, as if blown up like a balloon, and the victim may feel giddy and light-headed. Headache often develops during the night, so is present on waking, usually at the base or the posterior part of the head. If headache persists after exercise and taking two aspirin or paracetamol, the victim must descend. The severity of headache and its response to treatment, is often a measure of the severity of AMS, yet some people are found unconscious in the morning without any warning.

Fatigue – tiredness usually passes off with rest, fluids and food, all of which restore normal energy.

Appetite loss, nausea and indigestion – a farting tent-mate is odious; but gas problems improve with acclimatization.

Sleep disturbance – difficulty in falling asleep and frequent waking occur in the first week but may improve in the second. At great height it may never improve.

Shortness of breath on exertion (dyspnoea) – the chest feels uncomfortable and tight, but quiet easy breathing resumes after rest. A raspy cough, caused by the cold, dry air, is relieved by inhaling steam from a boiling pot.

Cheyne-Stokes periodic breathing is particularly noticeable and worrying at night. Breathing gradually deepens, is often accompanied by snoring and rises to a peak in four to five breaths; then it diminishes and finally ceases completely for several seconds so you may think the sleeper is dead. This alarming pattern then starts all over again. It is removed by taking acetazolamide (D.6.2).

Shortage of fluid (dehydration) – urine output is low for twenty-four hours with a story of not drinking enough and perhaps of exposure to heat and sun. Thirst rages, mucosae and tongue are dry (also caused by mouth breathing) and the pulse races. Changes in posture, for example sitting up having been lying down, cause the pulse to rise and a feeling of faintness.

Swelling – peripheral oedema makes the face puffy with bags under the eyes, rings on the fingers feel tight, and the ankles show the imprint of stocking elastic. Swelling is worst in the morning and wears off after rising.

   Act: rest, wait and see. Do not give oxygen because it may fool one into thinking the victim is better. If he has not improved within twenty-four hours, consider he has severe AMS, and **descend**.

   Mild AMS may blend unnoticed into severe AMS. HACO or HAPO become manifest depending on whether body-water settles in the brain or the lungs or both. The amount of peripheral oedema indicates the severity of AMS, so it is better to make a mistake by diagnosing the condition as severe and to descend, than to underestimate mild AMS.

Severe AMS

HIGH ALTITUDE CEREBRAL OEDEMA (HACO)
HACO usually occurs above 4,000 m (c 13,000 ft). Although less common than HAPO, in sixty per cent of cases victims will be suffering from both conditions. It appears as an exaggerated form of mild AMS, and as the symptoms of both conditions are similar it is often difficult to identify them.

Headache – severe, constant and throbbing like a bad toothache or migraine. No relief comes from paracetamol (D.1.1), codeine (D.1.3), a night's sleep, or massaging the temples.

Inco-ordination (ataxia) – the victim staggers as if drunk and fumbles fine movements, such as handling a camera. To distinguish ataxia from simple tiredness, make him perform the following tasks, comparing his actions with those of a normal person as a control:

Toe-to-heel walking: Walk placing the heel of one foot against the toes of the other along a straight line about 4 m long drawn in the snow or on the ground. If ataxic, he will sway and stagger and fall over when told to turn round and walk back.

Sitting upright without support; an ataxic person will roll over.

Languor – extreme fatigue is not reversed by rest. Pressure on the brain blunts the intellect. The victim won't talk, eat or drink; he lies curled up in a sleeping-bag avoiding contact with the outside world; he is apathetic and isolated, yet irritable and confused. If still active, he may show poor judgement and thus make bad mountaineering decisions. Sleep is fitful and punctuated by bad dreams. He may hallucinate, hear voices or see non-existent companions. He may be incontinent.

NB: Both ataxia and languor are common to hypothermia (take the rectal temperature), alcohol intoxication (smell the breath), and opiate drug abuse (look for pin-point pupils).

Vomiting – eventually vomiting leads to dehydration and the victim will be unable to replace fluid lost by drinking. Urine is scanty and dark yellow.

Eye signs: swelling of the optic nerve head (papilloedema), only visible with an ophthalmoscope by a skilled observer, signifies raised intracranial pressure within the skull and brain.

Coma – Finally the drowsy victim becomes unrousable, drifts into coma and may die. Convulsions are rare. Cerebral oedema victims can remain unconscious for days and yet recover completely.

This entire drama can unfold within hours and usually does so at night.

HIGH ALTITUDE RETINAL HAEMORRHAGE (HARH)
One third of all climbers going very high (above 6,000 m, c 20,000 ft) have haemorrhages in the retina at the back of the eye. The diagnosis requires an ophthalmoscope.

The haemorrhages look like red paint splashed on a wall. Usually there are no visible symptoms, however if the sensitive macula area, which interprets fine vision like reading, is involved a blurred or blank patch (scotoma) may be present in the central vision. These retinal haemorrhages heal in a few weeks and usually leave no scar. Similar haemorrhages tend to occur in the brain and may be more harmful.

HIGH ALTITUDE PULMONARY OEDEMA (HAPO)

In HAPO the lungs become water-logged hindering the passage of oxygen across the alveolar membranes into the blood, so the victim can drown in his own juices. HAPO is rare below 3,000 m, (c 10,000 ft). The condition develops thirty-six to seventy-two hours after arriving at altitude, and is cured by descent; rest and oxygen may help temporarily. HAPO affects children more than adults, but does not differentiate between the sexes. It may be related to severe exertion and rate of climb. The condition worsens at night when oxygen saturation is low owing to the quiet breathing of sleep, and periodic Cheyne-Stokes breathing which is exaggerated in HAPO. Those who have gone too high for their own good and have suffered HAPO before may suffer again and at a similar altitude.

Shortness of breath (dyspnoea) – occurs on slight exertion and is even present at rest. Breathing is irregular and fast at more than 25 breaths per minute. The victim does not improve with rest, and is hungry for air. The chest feels full and tight, but there is no actual pain which distinguishes it from heart attack or pneumonia.

Cough and sputum – early cough is tickling, hacking and dry, without sputum. Later the sputum is frothy because of air bubbling through oedema fluid in the alveoli, and pink with flecks of blood, because of capillary blood leaks and mild fever may be present. This can be distinguished from pneumonia or bronchitis where sputum is yellow-green owing to pus in the alveoli. The temperature will be high; more than 40° C (104° F).

Chest sounds – crackling, moist sounds (crepitations), like rubbing hair between finger and thumb beside the ear, can be heard with a stethoscope, or by placing an ear against the back of the victim's bare chest. The noise is due to air bubbling through fluid and can make a clearly audible rattling sound in both lungs, or on one side alone.

Cyanosis – the lips, face and finger-nails look blue at rest because haemoglobin is less saturated with oxygen than normal. A coloured tent will obscure cyanosis, which should be observed in natural light.

Pulse – will be rapid; more than 110 beats per minute.

The victim of severe AMS, whether of HACO or HAPO, may die quickly; so make a confident diagnosis, and act immediately and decisively.

Act: descend. Descent usually cures severe AMS miraculously. Immediate descent should not be delayed because of night, inconvenience, experimenting with drugs or oxygen, or in the hope of a mountain rescue team or helicopter – unless descending through difficult terrain in the dark is going to cause unwarranted danger to the whole party. The victim, always accompanied and perhaps carried, should descend at least 300 m, preferably 1,000 m. The greater and faster the descent, the more swiftly he will recover. Even a modest descent can save life. Once down, the victim should stay down until he can be examined by a wise physician.

The forms of treatment listed below play for time, but should never take preference over evacuating the victim immediately to a lower altitude. It is irrelevant that he just wants to lie in bed, sniff oxygen and drink tea; he needs to descend, if necessary by compulsion.

Rest – make the victim lie propped up, so oedema fluid sinks to the bottom of his lungs and pools in his legs. Keep him warm and relaxed; cold and anxiety aggravate AMS.

Oxygen – 100 per cent oxygen flowing at 6 litres per minute given via a tight-fitting mask is optimal, but settle for less if the supply is meagre. A change in the victim's colour from blue to pink shows that the oxygen is working. Oxygen may relieve headache and help pulmonary oedema, but it is no substitute for descent, merely an adjunct to it.

Fluids – drink enough (4–5 litres daily minimum) to maintain a plentiful flow of clear urine (1 litre daily minimum).

Drugs – clearly it is idiotic to plan an ascent so rapid that drugs must be relied on. However acetazolamide and dexamethasone taken in small doses are currently thought to reduce significantly the chance of getting AMS and the severity should it occur.

Acetazolamide (Diamox) (D.6.2) is a mild diuretic, that does not help acclimatization, but diminishes the incidence and severity of AMS, although useless in treatment. It also prevents or reduces AMS symptoms in people who have to ascend hurriedly to altitude, such as rescuers, if taken on the day of arrival at altitude, and for three days after. Finally it diminishes Cheyne-Stokes breathing and thereby improves the quality of sleep and maintains oxygenation in the newly arrived at altitude.

Rx: 500 mg slow-release capsule once daily.

Dexamethasone (Decadron) (D.4.2) a powerful steroid used in neurosurgery to shrink the brain. It may work by improving cerebral circulation which lowers intracranial pressure. Hence its beneficial effect in AMS and HACO.

Rx: 4 mg twice daily starting on the day of ascent and for three to five days thereafter for preventing AMS; for treating it Rx: 10 mg i/v then 4 mg six-hourly.

Frusemide (Lasix) (D.6.1) a powerful diuretic, which can lead to collapse from low volume shock if the victim is already dehydrated. Frusemide may clear the lungs of water in HAPO and reverse the suppression of urine brought on by altitude.

Rx: 40–120 mg by mouth, or 40 mg i/v slowly, daily.

Morphine (D.1.4) is a powerful analgesic which also allays the crippling anxiety of HAPO. Morphine dilates peripheral blood-vessels so blood is shifted away from the lungs thereby easing HAPO. It depresses breathing and must be used with caution in HAPO, and never in HACO.

Other drugs Digitalis is useless in HAPO as the victim is not in heart failure. Antibiotics are of value only in the presence of chest infection

with fever, pussy spit and crepitations. Antacids are unproven.
Tourniquets and intermittent-positive-pressure breathing have no place
in the outdoors.

With good sense Acute Mountain Sickness and its sinister offspring,
High Altitude Cerebral and Pulmonary Oedema, should not
happen. But if they do, descend rapidly to a lower altitude in order
to prevent their deadly consequences.

21 Immunization

N B: The specialized drugs mentioned in this chapter are mostly found only here and do not necessarily appear in the general drugs section on pages 24–27.

Travellers to tropical and sub-tropical countries can be protected by immunization against certain infectious diseases. Inoculation with a small amount of the organism that causes the disease, or a purified derivative of its toxin, produces immune antibodies, which protect against attacking organisms or their toxins.

Some vaccines require several doses spaced apart, therefore an immunization schedule should be planned three months ahead of intended departure. In emergency a crash course can be given in fifteen days. The local public health department will have up-to-date information on international immunization requirements.

IMMUNIZATIONS

Ideal schedule	week 1	2	3	4	5	6	7	8	9
Diphtheria/ tetanus		x							
Typhoid	x				x			x (optional)	
Cholera		x			x			x	
Polio	x								
Yellow Fever			x						
I.S.G.									x

Crash course	days	I	5	12	15
Diphtheria/ tetanus			x		
Typhoid			x	x	x
Cholera		x		x	x
Polio			x		
Yellow Fever		x			
I.S.G.					x

Anyone suffering from immuno-suppression, eczema or severe allergy, pregnant women, or those taking steroid medication (cortisone or prednisone) should avoid immunization. If wishing to travel they should obtain a certificate of exemption from their doctor.

Unexplained fever developing in the tropics, or soon after return therefrom, warrants consultation with a doctor, preferably one with access to knowledge about tropical diseases who can carry out screening, for example the London School of Hygiene and Tropical Medicine.

Immunizations to be considered

TETANUS AND DIPHTHERIA
These diseases are often fatal. Immunization gives complete protection, for which a sore, stiff arm and headache that lasts a couple of days is a small price to pay. Tetanus (lockjaw) still occurs in Britain and North America, although it is more common abroad.

All pre-school children should have been immunized so there will be few adults who have escaped primary immunization. Primary active immunization is obtained by two intramuscular injections spaced eight weeks apart. Protection lasts for ten years, then a booster dose is given. After a dirty wound or an animal bite a booster dose is given if there has been no immunization within the last five years, or if there is any doubt about a person being up-to-date with their shots.

Act: wounds should be thoroughly cleaned and dead tissue removed because tetanus spores lie dormant in the soil where horse and sheep manure abound. Tetanus should be treated in hospital with human tetanus immune globulin 3–10,000 U i/m with penicillin 1,000,000 U. four-hourly or tetracycline 500 mg six-hourly, each for five days.

TYPHOID

Two subcutaneous injections of vaccine prepared from killed bacteria, spaced four weeks apart. Have a booster dose if travelling to the tropics where typhoid is endemic. The injections may cause local soreness, headache, fever and malaise for a couple of days, during which time avoid alcohol. The vaccine is not fully protective; scrupulous hygiene with water, food and toilet is the only safeguard.

CHOLERA

Immunization is not recommended for tourists because the risk of cholera is low and the vaccine is poorly effective. Some countries, which should be checked with the public health authorities, demand a single dose for travellers from an infected area, and the international certificate is valid for six months only.

POLIOMYELITIS

Immunization is given to most schoolchildren and lasts a lifetime; it consists of three doses of trivalent (live) oral polio vaccine (OPV), or four doses of inactivated polio vaccine (IPV), with an IPV booster every five years until the age of eighteen. If travelling in places with an increased risk of polio, such as living rough in mountain huts with poor sanitation (polio virus is carried in faeces) anyone under forty should have a single booster dose of IPV (OPV for those under eighteen). Protection from polio is painless; the paralysing disease is deadly.

INFECTIOUS HEPATITIS

Immune serum globulin (ISG) 2 ml i/m is given for a visit of less than three months; 5 ml for longer. Protection is good for four months, only partial for a further two months against hepatitis A; it lasts for six months and should be repeated if the danger of infection persists. ISG should be given after other immunizations because it interferes with antibody formation, upon which their effectiveness depends.

Hepatitis A virus is carried in faeces and is acquired from infected food and water, or by swimming near a sewage outlet. Jaundice is preceded for three to seven days by vague, unpleasant malaise. Rest is the only treatment.

The new hepatitis B vaccine is recommended for travellers to highly endemic areas like South-east Asia and sub-Saharan Africa, or those likely to come in contact with blood or secretions of potentially infected persons.

TUBERCULOSIS

BCG immunization is given only to high-risk groups such as medical personnel who have a negative tuberculin (Mantoux) skin test.

MEASLES

Anyone born after 1956 who has not had measles, or who has not had the vaccine, should receive a single 1 ml dose.

YELLOW FEVER

Immunization is advisable before travelling to infected areas (the forests of Central and South America, and East, Central and West Africa); some countries demand vaccination for travellers from these areas. The live virus can only be obtained from officially designated centres and an International Certificate is valid ten days after immunization and lasts for ten years.

Yellow fever used to be a common killer, but is now quite rare. It is carried by mosquitos from mammals, principally monkeys, to man.

SMALLPOX

Vaccination should no longer be given because smallpox has been eradicated world-wide. But several countries still insist on a valid International Certificate showing vaccination within the previous three years.

RABIES

Immunization is only recommended for travellers anticipating contact with rabies-bearing animals, or those going into an area where rabies is a constant threat (see page 238).

MALARIA

No immunization is possible against malaria which is caused by mosquito-borne parasites, Plasmodium falciparum, P. vivax, P. malariae, and P. ovale. Travellers to endemic areas below an altitude of 1,200 m should take [chloroquine] 300 mg base (500 mg salt) once weekly from one week before arrival until six weeks after leaving the endemic area.

In some places chloroquine-resistant P. falciparum exists, details of which should be obtained from the consulates of the countries to which a visit is planned, or the local malaria reference centres. Travellers to chloroquine-resistant areas should take [pyrimethamine] 25 mg and [sulfadoxine] (Fansidar) 500 mg once weekly in addition to chloroquine 500 mg, but be aware that Fansidar can cause serious (even lethal) skin complications.

Mosquitoes tend to bite around dusk, but are discouraged by long sleeves, trousers, insect repellent and by mosquito netting over beds. It only takes one bite from an infected mosquito to pass on malaria, so there is risk even on a brief stop-over in a malarial area. The only protection is common sense. Anti-malarial drugs only suppress the parasite; they must be taken regularly in order to maintain an effective blood concentration, and are not one hundred per cent effective.

Malaria attacks are heralded by mild fever and sore muscles, followed in several days by chills and high fever. The victim shivers so violently the bed shakes, teeth chatter, skin is blue and cold, the pulse races and the victim feels cold. An hour later he becomes hot with a temperature of up to 41° C (107° F), is flushed, suffers severe headache and may be delirious. Then the temperature falls, he sweats profusely and feels better again. This cycle may be repeated every one, two or three days. The parasite can be demonstrated under the microscope.

Act: cool the victim. Push fluids to maintain a urine output of more than 1 litre per twenty-four hours.

Rx: [chloroquine phosphate] 600 mg base (1 g salt) immediately, then 300 mg base (500 mg salt) after six hours, then 300 mg base per day for two days. Follow-up with [primaquine phosphate] is advised to prevent relapses in P. vivax and P. ovale infections only; Rx: 26.3 mg daily for two weeks.

Hygiene

Water and food are the most common sources of disease because of pollution by infected faeces and urine of disease carriers, for example in typhoid, shigella and cholera. People in tropical countries are generally less discriminating about where they defecate, partly owing to ignorance, partly to lack of adequate latrines. Food and drinking water become contaminated directly, or by flies. Disease is prevented by drinking pure water only, eating clean food and disposing of sewage efficiently.

WATER

Hillside springs, clear of human habitation and animal grazing, should be safe for drinking, but stream and river water is probably polluted. Glacial mud and mica, that give alpine rivers their murky appearance, often upset the gut.

All water outside Europe and North America, even in hotels and restaurants, should be considered unsafe to drink unless it has been boiled; kitchens are probably only as clean as the toilets. If in doubt about drinking water, purify it yourself and only drink boiled water, or tea or coffee made with boiling water. Avoid drinking tap water or using it for brushing teeth. Certain towns, such as Kathmandu, have notoriously polluted civil water supplies.

Water purification – Boiling: a few seconds' brisk boiling kills most organisms; boiling for ten minutes kills amoeba cysts and hepatitis virus, the only way water can be sterilized properly. The colour, taste and smell of water is immaterial provided it has been adequately boiled. This may be difficult at high altitude where the boiling point is lower than at sea-level.
– Chemical treatment: [tincture of iodine] 2 per cent (5 drops per litre for clear water, 10 drops for cold or cloudy water, allowed to stand for thirty minutes) kills giardia and amoeba cysts, as well as bacteria. [Chlorine] (10 drops of 1 per cent solution to 1 litre of

water) is the basic ingredient of liquid laundry bleach and some water-purifying tablets; it kills most water-borne bacteria, but not amoeba cysts or bacteria embedded in solid particles. When large volumes of water have to be purified and boiling is not practicable, commercial chlorine or iodine bought across the counter will do. The water must be treated for fifteen minutes to one hour. A pinch of salt added to each litre improves the taste.

– Filtration: removes suspended matter and some bacteria, giving the water a deceptively clear appearance. Some filters use an ion exchange resin, and though useful for cleaning large volumes of water, are the least reliable way of making it pure. Filters have to be kept scrupulously clean or they lose their effectiveness. Water should be boiled after filtration, not before.

DRINKS

Bottled fizz, ice cubes, and ice lollipops are only as safe as the water from which they are made. Unpasteurized milk must be boiled; powdered milk is only safe if made up with boiled water and stored in a refrigerator. Wine drunk in moderation is harmless, but a surfeit upsets the stomach. Contrary to legend, alcoholic spirits do not sterilize the gut.

ICE CREAM

Germs are harboured in ice-cream, both from the ingredients and from subsequent handling. Well-advertised brands with a reputation at stake, should be reasonably safe.

FOOD

Freshly- and thoroughly-cooked food is safe because bacteria are killed by heat. Avoid pre-cooked and handled food, especially where flies abound. Peel all fruit and vegetables; thorough washing is only second best so beware of salads, tomatoes, lettuces and watercress because human night-soil is often used as a fertilizer in the tropics. Meat should be thoroughly cooked and eaten immediately because raw or under-done beef and pork harbour tapeworms. Beware of inadequately cleaned prawns and shell-fish which live on sewage and concentrate the organisms.

Strike a balance between worrying obsessively about what you eat and drink, and common-sense precaution. Some early contact with germs and the accompanying dose of the runs is inevitable; immunity gained may protect against further attacks.

PERSONAL HYGIENE
Many toilets are dirty; squatters have to keep balance by holding onto the walls. Take toilet paper because newsprint is rough and fragile, and glossy magazines are impossible. Wash hands carefully with soap and water immediately afterwards. Keep nails short and clean.

Gut problems

Gastro-enteritis, or food-poisoning, causes diarrhoea, which means liquid stools; dysentery is diarrhoea with blood. Acute diarrhoea may follow an influenzal-virus illness, or pigging-out on certain foods.

TRAVELLERS' DIARRHOEA
This causes more trouble than all other medical hazards encountered abroad. It has as many local names (Gippy Tummy, Delhi Belly, Kathmandu Quickstep, Tokyo Trots, Rangoon Runs, Montezuma's Revenge) as patent remedies. The causes may include gluttony, change in climate and an upset in bacteria that are normal and necessary in the bowel. Infection may occur with disease-causing organisms carried in water and food, for example enterotoxigenic Escherichia coli and shigella, less commonly with salmonella and other bacteria and viruses. Diarrhoea developing weeks after return from abroad may be due to the protozoa Giardia lamblia.

Wise doctors recommend hygiene rather than drugs to prevent travellers' diarrhoea. Much pleasure in travelling abroad comes from eating local food and drinking wine; it is hardly worth going so far for beer, fish and chips. But be moderate to avoid what could be a very expensive and distressing upset gut.

In exceptional circumstances take [doxycycline], a long-acting tetracycline; 100 mg daily for three weeks from the day before departure. It is expensive and has several unpleasant side-effects, such as sunlight sensitivity. It reduces the person's own bacterial flora and may increase the risk of more serious enteric infections such as salmonella.

Travellers' diarrhoea is usually an acute, explosive, self-limiting illness that is accompanied by vomiting and feeling groggy because of dehydration from loss of body-water. It clears in several days.

Act: go to bed and drink unlimited fluids; at least 500 ml an hour of plain boiled water. Eat moderately; dried toast or peeled, grated apple turned brown (pecten) may help to solidify the stools. A short period of starvation in a well-nourished person does no harm, but some travellers living on a shoe-string and climbers after their climb may be malnourished so further starvation will not help.

Fluid loss: if diarrhoea becomes severe with loss of large volumes of water and necessarily electrolytes, as in cholera, the person may rapidly become dehydrated. Fluid can be replaced according to the WHO formula (D.18), which can be made up by any pharmacist (see page 41). Sip one glass (250 ml) for each bowel movement, or more if still thirsty or if the urine is scanty or yellow and concentrated. If less than ten watery stools are passed a day drink 1–2 litres every twenty-four hours; if more than ten, sip 1–2 litres every six hours. On an expedition abroad carry several packets of ready-measured powder, of which many commercial preparations are available.

Anti-motility drugs: slow the gut's peristaltic contractions and ease diarrhoea and cramping pains, but a bacterial illness may be prolonged because they slow excretion of bacteria and toxins. Most are related to the narcotic drugs so may cause drowsiness. Do not use for more than 2–3 days.

Rx: codeine phosphate (D.1.3) 15–30 mg eight-hourly, loperamide (D.9.3) 4 mg eight-hourly; these two can be given together.

Antibiotics: should not be used blindly because they kill normal bacteria, which are necessary for gut function, as well as toxin-producing bacteria; also they encourage antibiotic-resistant strains of E. coli to emerge. Antibiotics play little part in speeding recovery and they may prolong the excretion of bacteria during convalescence. The risk of using them prophylactically may outweigh the benefits.

If severe diarrhoea (more than six stools per day), does not stop after twenty-four to forty-eight hours on this treatment, or if blood appears in the stools, go to a hospital for a stool examination.

Rx: co-trimoxazole (D.2.2) 1–2 tabs twelve-hourly for three to five days. If diarrhoea persists nonetheless, presume it may be due to giardia, and Rx: metronidazole (D.2.3) 250 mg eight-hourly for a week.

Other medicines: many popular brands of diarrhoea medicine are, at best, useless (Kaopectate alters the consistency of the stool and relieves discomfort for those who have to keep moving); at worst, dangerous (iodohydroxyquin (Entero-vioform) can cause blindness). Avoid them.

SHIGELLOSIS (bacillary dysentery)
This condition has a sudden severe onset with urgent, explosive diarrhoea that may contain blood, mucus and pus, and causes griping abdominal cramps. The temperature and pulse rate rise quickly. The victim has shivering rigors and feels sick, but usually does not vomit. Shigellosis is similar clinically to amoebic dysentery (see below) and can only be diagnosed accurately by culturing the offending shigella organism from the stool. Antibiotic sensitivity can then be tested and the appropriate drug prescribed.

Prevent shigella by taking all the measures described above for travellers' diarrhoea; but do not use anti-motility drugs which can intensify the illness and delay excretion of toxic organisms.

Rx: co-trimoxazole (D.2.2), [amoxycillin] or [chloramphenicol] 250 mg eight-hourly is empirical treatment.

CHOLERA
A rare disease now, it is spread by faecally contaminated water and raw shellfish. Sudden onset of profuse, watery diarrhoea with cramps and collapse due to dehydration (sometimes within a few hours) in a known epidemic area is cause to suspect cholera. Fluids and electrolytes must be replaced urgently.

TYPHOID (enteric fever)
Fever increases with rapid temperature fluctuations over one to
three weeks and may reach 40° C (104° F). There is vague
abdominal pain and cough. Constipation at first may, on rare
occasions, turn to bloody, pea-soup diarrhoea. Less common
symptoms are headache, a flushed face and rose-coloured spots on
the trunk. Eventually the victim becomes prostrate and desperately
ill.

Rx: [chloramphenicol], the drug of choice, 500 mg six-hourly for
two weeks, but it has serious side-effects so should only be
administered after reaching a bacteriological diagnosis.
Co-trimoxazole (D.2.2) 2 tabs six-hourly or [amoxycillin] 2 g
six-hourly are second choice. Under medical supervision only,
prednisone (D.4.1) 10 mg six-hourly for a week reduces symptoms
and the likelihood of the dangerous complication of perforation of
the bowel.

Parasites

AMOEBIASIS (Entamoeba histolytica)
Dysentery may develop gradually over a month but the majority of
infected persons are asymptomatic carriers. At the start, three to
four loose, foul-smelling stools are passed daily; this increases to a
dozen with blood flecks, slimy mucus, painful straining and colicky
pain on the right side of the abdomen. Liver abscess is a dreaded
late complication, but usually not related to an attack of amoebic
dysentery.

Rx: metronidazole (D.2.3) 750 mg eight-hourly for one week.

GIARDIASIS (Giardia lamblia)
Crampy diarrhoea persisting after the return of a traveller is
suspicious. Beavers and many other wild and domestic animals
carry the parasite and infect surface water supplies. If not treated
diarrhoea may become chronic with malabsorption, weight loss,
and upper abdominal pain like peptic ulcer or gall-bladder disease.

Rx: metronidazole (D.2.3) 250 mg eight-hourly for one week.
Avoid alcohol.

WORMS

Worms are a chronic cause of ill-health in the tropics and can be prevented by careful hygiene. Usually one dose of the appropriate drug cleans out the worm, the ova of which must be identified by microscopy of the stool.

Round worm (ascaris), thread or pin worm (enterobius), and whipworm (trichuris) – the worms, or part of them, may be seen in the stool. An itchy bum is sometimes the first warning of enterobius. Worms can mimic appendicitis, which is a rare disease in natives of the tropics, so surgeons should go easy on the knife.
   Rx: [mebendazole] 100 mg twice daily for three days.

Tapeworm (taenia) and diphyllobothrium – thrive in under-cooked beef, pork and fish. Segments of the worm are passed in the stool, but the head remains attached to the gut and must be killed to prevent it growing into another worm.
   Rx: [niclosamide] 2 g in two doses an hour apart, while fasting.

Hookworm (ankylostoma) and strongyloides – larvae enter through abrasions on the feet, so wear shoes in infected regions. Anaemia may result from heavy and chronic infections.
   Rx: [mebendazole] 100 mg twice daily for three days.

Schistosomiasis (bilharzia) – the infective stage of this fluke lives in fresh water and enters the body through unbroken skin, so beware of drinking from, or paddling or swimming in, slow-flowing rivers or lakes. The veins of the bladder and intestine are its favourite haunt, so blood may be passed in the urine.
   Rx: [praziquantel] 40 mg/kg body weight as a single oral dose.

Any bite, including human bites, must immediately be washed with plenty of soap and water because mouths are full of bacteria. Any sign of infection – redness around the wound, or enlarged, tender neighbouring lymph glands – should be treated with an antibiotic. Check the victim's tetanus immunization is up-to-date; if not, remind him to get a booster dose soon.

Animal bites

RABIES

The possibility of rabies should be considered after an animal bite, especially in the tropics or in an endemic area. Although rare, rabies is always lethal. Dogs are the commonest vectors, but foxes, the wolf family, skunks, racoons and bats can all carry rabies; rabbits, squirrels, chipmunks, rats and mice never do. Rabies virus lives in the saliva of an infected animal, whose nervous system becomes affected causing the frothing of mad dogs; the virus enters humans through a break in the skin, or possibly by breathing the air in caves inhabited by rabid bats. Most domestic animals in the western world are immunized against rabies; not so in the tropics.

Prevention – if bitten or licked by a suspect animal, wash the wound liberally with soap and water. Leave it open to the sun because ultra-violet light kills some viruses. Cage any suspect animal, if not possible, shoot it. If the animal is alive and free of rabies after ten days, the victim of the bite is safe; if it develops signs of rabies kill it and send the head, carefully wrapped, to a laboratory for examination of the brain. If the result is positive for rabies, or immediately after the bite of a known rabid animal, start a course of anti-rabies vaccine. Once rabies is manifest with painful spasms (especially on swallowing, causing hatred of water – hydrophobia) and excitement leading to convulsions and paralysis, there is no hope of recovery.

Rx: [rabies immune globulin (RIG)] 20 IU/kg in one dose as soon as possible after exposure plus [human diploid cell vaccine (HDCV)] 1 ml i/m at different sites on days 0, 3, 7, 14, 28, and 90.

TULAREMIA

This condition is caused by handling diseased or dead rabbits and beavers. When the organism is inoculated by thorns and briars it develops ulcers and enlarged lymph glands. Seek medical advice.

Snake bites

Less than one in twenty people bitten by snakes die from snake-bite poisoning. In Britain the only poisonous snakes are common vipers (adders); grass snakes are harmless. Vipers have two fangs, so look for puncture marks before presuming a bite. North America has pit vipers (rattlesnakes, cotton-mouths, copper-heads) and coral snakes.

Viper venom can cause an immediate, painful, stinging inflammation at the bite site and tissue sloughing. Occasionally a severe body reaction occurs with shock; chills, vomiting, convulsions. Breathing and kidney failure follow. Coral snakes rarely bite, but if they do the reaction may be delayed twelve hours, when the victim suddenly collapses. Cobras and many deadly snakes abound in the tropics, so consult an appropriate book.

When in a snake area wear boots, carry a stick and a flashlight at night and examine clothes, footwear and sleeping-bag before climbing in. Snakes only attack when frightened or provoked. If possible kill the snake without damaging identifying marks around the head; pick up the head cautiously because it can strike up to an hour after being cut off. Take the snake's head and the victim to the local hospital, which may keep anti-venom against local varieties of poisonous snakes.

Act: wash the bite thoroughly with soap and water. Do not suck or slash the skin over the bite, or pee on it. Bandage firmly and tightly over the bite around the entire limb, splint it, and keep it hanging down in order to reduce venom entering the blood-stream. Do not freeze or use tourniquets, which can lead to gangrene of the limb. If cobra venom has been spat into the eyes wash them with plenty of water.

Rx: [antivenom] 50 ml–400 ml immediately, depending on the severity of the poison. Be sure the victim has actually been bitten because horse serum, from which the antivenom is made, can cause grave hypersensitivity reactions and anaphylactic shock. Treat pain and give reassurance because a snake-bite strikes terror to the heart. Give a tetanus booster if not up-to-date. Do not use antibiotics unless infection follows.

SCORPIONS, SPIDERS, CATERPILLARS, CENTIPEDES AND LEGION OTHER CREEPY-CRAWLIES

Bites may be venomous causing symptoms varying from local pain to shock and collapse. Dust 10 per cent DDT powder in places like outhouse seats where the beasties may lurk and give a nasty bite.

Rx: similar to snake-bite. Antivenom is available against scorpions and spiders (Black Widow). Local anaesthetic injected into the site may ease the pain.

Insect bites

BEES, WASPS AND HORNETS

Stings can be painful and unpleasant. They can also kill a sensitive or allergic person by anaphylaxis, a reaction which causes giant welts (urticaria), severe wheezing, tight chest, stridorous choking and shock. Such people should be skin tested; if they are positive and have had a severe reaction before, they should have venom de-sensitizing injections (which may themselves cause a grave allergic reaction) every four weeks indefinitely during the season. They should wear a Medic-alert medallion, and carry a kit containing 2 ampoules of adrenaline 0.3 ml of 1:1,000 solution in pre-loaded syringes with a needle attached.

Rx: for severe allergy or anaphylaxis: adrenaline (D.7.2) 1:1,000, 0.3 ml i/v (slowly), s/c, or i/m, if in severe shock, repeated every half-hour. Beware: adrenaline can cause the pulse to race and beat irregularly.

for the sting: remove it with tweezers, apply a hot compress. Neutralize the venom; bee venom is acid so apply bicarbonate of soda or weak ammonia, wasp venom is alkaline so use vinegar or lemon juice. Anti-histamines (D.3) ease the itch.

MOSQUITOES AND BLACK FLIES

Mosquitoes are described under Malaria (see page 229). Black flies, 'no-see-ums', thrive in the sub-Arctic. They penetrate mosquito netting and give a vicious bite out of proportion to their tiny size. Danger comes from infection of the bites because of wild scratching.

SCABIES, LICE, NITS, FLEAS AND BED BUGS

Scabies mites burrow under the skin of the trunk and limbs (everywhere excluding the face), causing intense itching, worse at night in a warm bed. Tiny red spots are visible at the bite, and scratch marks are all over the body. Lice (pediculus) lay eggs (nits), which are cemented to the hair of the head and pubis and in clothing seams. Fleas cause intense itching and leave a trail of bites around the midriff. Bed bugs bite and smell, but do not carry disease.

Rx: [malathion]. For scabies apply one thin layer of the lotion all over the body excluding the face, leave it for twenty-four hours, then shower. Repeat once in a week if necessary, or use [benzyl benzoate] nightly for three nights. Hot wash all clothes and bedding, air sleeping-bags in the sun, and treat the family or tent-mates likewise.

For lice do a single shampoo of one tablespoonful for four minutes, then rinse and dry.

ITCHING

Itching can drive a person crazy, literally; more scratch, more itch and dirty finger-nails will turn a bite septic.

Rx: [calamine] the lotion soothes and cools more than the cream.

starch or oatmeal paste. Add 1 cup to 1 litre of boiling water and apply the paste when cool to the area.

anti-histamines quell itching, promethazine (D.3.1) most strongly but cause drowsiness, chlorpheniramine (D.3.2) the least soporific. Anti-histamine creams can sensitize the skin to oral anti-histamines taken later and a violent skin reaction may result.

betamethasone (D.11.1) steroid cream, use only if other methods fail.

INSECT REPELLENTS
Applied to the skin they repel insects for four hours maximum.

Rx: an insect repellent containing DET (diethyltoluamide), or DMP (dimethylphthalate).

INSECTICIDES
The clothing and the person wearing it must be treated. Crystals of powder or droplets of spray stick to the insect and slowly paralyse it.

Rx: an insectide containing DDT (dicophane).

ALLERGY
A sensitivity reaction to foreign protein may manifest as simply local swelling with welts and occasionally some wheezing.

Rx: anti-histamine (D.3).

LEECHES AND TICKS
Leeches are troublesome in rain forests and tropical marshes. The first sign may be a bootful of blood at the end of the day, because bites are painless and prevent blood clotting. Leeches find their way into laced boots, so open sandals have the advantage that you can see them early and deal with them. A flick of a finger, a touch of salt, a lighted cigarette, or [tincture of iodine] makes the leech drop off; do not pull them or the head will be left in the wound and continue to irritate. Clean the wound with soap and water, and press to stop bleeding.

JELLYFISH, STINGRAYS, SEA ANEMONES
Stings from these sea creatures cause intense burning pain, local swelling, and red weals. Sometimes the victim is prostrated.

Rx: as for other bites.

Sexually transmitted diseases

Unfortunately the aphorism 'once bitten twice shy' does not always apply to foreign travellers; the excitement and availability of commercial sex away from home may cause them to abandon discretion. Some nasty strains of penicillin-resistant gonococci (which cause gonorrhoea), treponema (which cause syphylis) and herpes virus exist abroad. AIDS (auto-immune deficiency syndrome) can no longer be considered a unisexual disease and fifty per cent of people, male and female, in some African countries have the HIV antibody. AIDS is also acquired from unsterile injections (particularly in intravenous drug users) and blood transfusions.

Act: don't, it's safer that way. But if caught with your pants down and if a pussy urethral discharge and painful peeing come on while in the mountains, following an unwise sexual contact on the way in, get to a V.D. specialist clinic quickly.

Rx: [amoxycillin] 500 mg eight-hourly for ten days, or cephalosporin (D.2.1).

Index